CONTENTS

Ships in Focus Publications
Correspondence and editorial:
Roy Fenton
18 Durrington Avenue, London SW20 8NT
020 8879 3527
rfenton@rfenton.demon.co.uk

Orders and photographic:
John & Marion Clarkson
18 Franklands, Longton, Preston PR4 5PD
01772 612855
sales@shipsinfocus.co.uk
© 2003 Individual contributors, John Clarkson and Roy Fenton.

Printed by Amadeus Press Ltd., Cleckheaton, Yorkshire.
Designed by Hugh Smallwood, John Clarkson and Roy Fenton.
SHIPS IN FOCUS RECORD
ISBN 1 901703 72-X

SHIPS IN FOCUS
December

Like all editors, we like getting letters. They tell us that readers appreciate what we provide, they give us a feel for which features are most popular, and put us right when we or our contributors err with facts. Perhaps most importantly, they cast fresh light on events, a classic example being William Riddell's letter about building the *City of Melbourne* in this issue's 'Putting the Record Straight.'

It is Ships in Focus' policy to reply to or acknowledge every letter or e-mail we receive at our London editorial address. However, readers should remember that our business is very much a cottage industry. Yes, it is electronic cottages from which we work, but there are very few workers in the cottages to handle correspondence. Often, it comes down to deciding between replying to the most recent mail or ensuring this journal or another publication gets to the printer on time.

So, dear reader, if you have written to the Editor and not received a reply, do not despair: one will almost certainly arrive sooner or, more probably, later. We believe that fully 95 percent of letters we have ever received have been replied to. In this we may have a better record than contemporary journals. When we invited several editors of shipping magazines to a book launch, only one bothered to reply. If this happens between editors, who might be expected to have some fellow feeling, what are these journal's records for replying to readers?

So please keep the letters and e-mails coming to the editorial address. If, like most correspondents, you have something worthwhile to add or correct, the chances are great that your letter will appear in 'Putting the Record Straight'. And yes, you will receive a reply or acknowledgement. Eventually.

Opposite are details of a major book published jointly by the World Ship Society and Ships in Focus, which is available to *Record* subscribers and to WSS members at a special price. It is another good reason for subscribing to *Record,* or for joining the WSS; but please note: if you do both (which we strongly advise) you will not qualify for two discounts!

SUBSCRIPTION RATES FOR RECORD

Readers can start their subscription with any issue, and are welcome to backdate it to receive previous issues.

	3 issues	4 issues
UK	£23	£31
Europe (airmail)	£25	£34
Rest of world (surface mail)	£25	£34
Rest of world (airmail)	£30	£40

Beaverelm. See page 73. *[World Ship Photo Library]*

CP Explorer leaves Rotterdam after conversion to a container ship (see page 72). *[Gercofoto, Rotterdam, courtesy Peter Newall]*

CANADIAN PACIFIC'S BEAVERS: Part 2
Stephen Howells

The eight Beavers featured in the first part of this article were all designed for Canadian Pacific's services. In contrast, only two of the further nine ships which were to carry Beaver names were built to the company's specification, the others being second hand acquisitions.

Fast cargo liners
Three ships acquired in the late 1940s and early 1950s were standard fast cargo liners built for the Ministry of War Transport. As the editors intend to devote a full feature in a future *Record* to these impressive ships, it will suffice to record here that Canadian Pacific bought two direct from the Ministry in 1946, with a third coming from Furness, Withy in October 1952. With the four ships ordered during wartime (detailed in the first part of this article), this gave a fleet of seven cargo ships by 1952, which between them completed 43 transatlantic voyages in that year. The additional ship, plus the return of the *Maplecove* and *Mapledell* from the unsuccessful Pacific service, allowed Rotterdam and Hamburg to be reinstated as ports of call in 1953 and 1954. The original pair of Empires had accommodation for 35 passengers, but this was reduced to 12 in 1948.

The unique *Beaverbrae*
The third post-war acquisition was a very different vessel. The second *Beaverbrae* was the only Beaver to carry substantial numbers of passengers - over 700, a remarkable number considering her modest accommodation block - and the only one to fly the Canadian flag. A captured German ship allocated to Canada as war reparations, she was used to carry some of the many refugees from wartime Europe whom the Canadian government accepted for resettlement. Eastbound, she carried only cargo, which is probably why the company gave her a Beaver name: she hardly qualified to be an 'Empress' along with the company's major passenger ships. When much of her refugee work was over, *Beaverbrae* was sold in November 1954, but continued to have a colourful and adventurous career which is detailed below.

To the Great Lakes
Oddly, Canadian Pacific had left trading to the Great Lakes to such as Manchester Liners and the Norwegian-Dutch venture Fjell-Orange Line, who used small ships suited to the locks above Montreal. With the St. Lawrence Seaway due to open and allow full-sized ocean ships access to the Great Lakes, Canadian Pacific could not ignore its potential any longer. In 1957 they began chartering ships to offer services from London and Liverpool, taking bigger vessels when the Seaway opened in 1959. It was not until 1961 that a company-owned vessel sailed on the Great Lakes service, the small *Beaverfir*. It seems the older and larger Beavers did not visit the Great Lakes, and all of these were sold by 1963. Canadian Pacific was now relying heavily on tonnage chartered from Norwegian and German owners. Many chartered ships carried the company's funnel and a few were renamed - the *Medicine Hat*, ex-*Anders Rogenaes* and *Moose Jaw* ex-*N.O. Rogenaes* being particularly memorable - but none carried a Beaver name.

Canadian Pacific were instrumental in inaugurating a year-round service to the ice-bound ports in Quebec, initially experimenting with chartered ice-strengthened ships. Indeed, the writer was an unwitting witness to this experiment, and remembers being astonished to see the Canada Steamship's *Eskimo* at Ellesmere Port on the Mersey in the early 1960s. The significance of the sighting of this very unusual visitor only dawned on me when researching this feature. With this experience, Canadian Pacific ordered an ice-strengthened ship, the *Beaverpine*. Two further small ships were bought from Norwegian owners in 1962 and 1963.

Containers and the end of Beavers
With their railroad interests, it was natural that Canadian Pacific should want to experiment with containers, which could be readily transferred between ship and rail. Again, they started cautiously, and to a daily Montreal to Toronto passenger train was added a flat car to carry a container and container-friendly ships were chartered in. The result was the order for the *Beaveroak*, designed to carry containers although not dispensing with cargo gear.

Sadly, *Beaveroak* was to be the last ship given a Beaver name. When the company's transatlantic trade was fully containerised with the delivery of three new ships in 1971, two remaining *Beavers* were themselves converted to gearless container carriers, but lost their names. The 'Beaver' theme was, it has to be said, slightly artificial, but the names had a certain resonance, and a strong identity with Canada and with Canadian Pacific's forebears on the Atlantic. None of this could be said for the new names. *CP Explorer* and *CP Ambassador* must have been chosen by accountants (or, worse, management consultants) with no poetry in their souls. The Canadian Pacific story was to have a number of further twists and turns, but the saga of the Beavers ended in the early 1970s. The first two generations of Beavers had been fine, innovative and impressive ships, and if the third generation were less notable there was interest in their diversity. With their demise in the 1970s, the North Atlantic shipping scene became a little duller.

BEAVERBURN (2)
Caledon Shipbuilding and Engineering Co. Ltd., Dundee; 1944, 9,875gt, 476 feet
Two steam turbines double-reduction geared to one shaft by C.A. Parsons Ltd., Newcastle-upon-Tyne

Even after taking delivery of their four Beavers ordered during wartime, Canadian Pacific needed more ships, their pre-war fleet having been completely wiped out during the conflict. The next best thing to their own ships were the standard 15-knot, turbine-driven cargo liners built for the British Government. Two were bought as soon as they became available in May 1946, *Empire Captain* becoming the second *Beaverburn*.

After 14 years of apparently trouble-free service *Beaverburn*, along with one of her sisters, was sold in 1960 to Ben Line. This canny Scots company was acquiring fast, if not necessarily modern, cargo ships to keep up with their competitors whilst avoiding high levels of investment in vessels which would sooner or later be made redundant by containerisation. As *Bennachie* she worked for four years on Far Eastern services before being sold to an owner who was himself Far Eastern, W. H. Eddie Hsu of Taiwan and who renamed her *Silvana* under the Liberian flag. She was broken up, also in Taiwan, during April and May 1971.

The photographs on this

spread show that only two of the three Beavers had the cowl-topped funnel.

[Top and middle: J. and M. Clarkson; bottom: Roy Fenton collection]

BEAVERFORD (2)
Caledon Shipbuilding and Engineering Co. Ltd., Dundee; 1944, 9,881gt, 476 feet
Two steam turbines double-reduction geared to one shaft by Metropolitan Vickers Electrical Co. Ltd., Manchester.
The former *Empire Kitchener*, *Beaverford* was to have the longest career with Canadian Pacific of their three standard fast cargo liners. After 17 years on the North Atlantic, in 1963 she was sold to P.S. Li, a Hong Kong-based entrepreneur who must win the prize for the shipowner with the shortest name, for whom she ran under the Panama flag as *Hulda*. In 1966 she passed without change of name to another Chinese gentleman, Y.C. Cheng, but this time New York-based. At Gulfport during August 1968, *Hulda* broke her moorings during a hurricane and went aground at Camille, Mississipi. The 24-year-old ship was declared a constructive total loss and was broken up on the spot. [*J. and M. Clarkson*]

BEAVERLODGE
Furness Shipbuilding Co. Ltd., Haverton Hill-on-Tees; 1943, 9,904gt, 476 feet
Two steam turbines double reduction geared to a single shaft by Richardsons, Westgarth and Co. Ltd., Hartlepool.
Clearly pleased with *Beaverburn* and *Beaverlodge*, Canadian Pacific looked round for another of these turbine-engined craft and in October 1952 paid a hefty £800,000 for a nine year-old example, *Zealandic*. She had been built as *Empire Regent* at the Furness yard on the Tees where the type had been largely designed, and after wartime management by Brocklebanks had been bought by the Furness group, becoming first *Black Prince* and later *Zealandic* for charter to Shaw, Savill.
Her Canadian Pacific career was relatively short, and in 1960 she passed with *Beaverburn* to Ben Line, becoming *Benhiant*. The sale price was just £150,000, a bargain for Ben who got a good ten years' service from her. The inevitable flag of convenience operator, who renamed her *Venus* in 1970, had her for only a year before delivering her to the Kaohsiung breakers in April 1971.
[*A. Duncan, courtesy George Scott*]

HUASCARAN, BEAVERBRAE (2) and AURELIA

Blohm und Voss A.G., Hamburg; 1937, 9,034g, 488 feet
Two 8-cyl and one 6-cyl. oil engines, both 2SCSA with electric drive by Blohm und Voss A.G., Hamburg

Seeing a major war, several rebuilds and a serious fire, this ship certainly had a career that was eventful, and long. She was built as *Huascaran* for the West Coast of South America service of Hamburg-Amerika, the outbreak of the Second World War meaning she worked for barely two years on this route. As a submarine depot ship in the Baltic, she seems to have come through the conflict unscathed, and was duly captured by the Allies and allocated to the Canadian Government as a war reparation. Before crossing the Atlantic for her new owners she underwent a much-needed dry docking at Liverpool, where she was photographed by John McRoberts on 26th April 1947 (top). Readers' opinions are sought on the purpose of what appears to be lifting gear rigged on her forecastle.

On reaching Canada, the Government sold her in September 1947 to Canadian Pacific, and she was reconditioned at Sorel emerging in February 1948 as *Beaverbrae* with accommodation for 74 cabin passengers and almost 700 in dormitories (middle). As recorded above, she carried refugees and cargo westbound, and cargo only eastbound, averaging eight voyages each year, many of which terminated at Bremerhaven, Bremen or Antwerp. In November 1954 *Beaverbrae* was sold to Italian owners, Cogedar Line of Genoa.

The ship's fourth career was as an Australian emigrant ship, for which she was further rebuilt, with accommodation for a total of 1,126 'tourist' class passengers and many more boats (bottom). As *Aurelia* her route was Rotterdam and Southampton via Suez to Fremantle, Melbourne and Sydney, with some additional calls on the return voyage. She was re-engined in 1959 and further rebuilt in 1963, by when her clientele were more likely to be tourists than emigrants. After an unsuccessful attempt to use *Aurelia* in the British cruise market, she was sold to Chandris in 1968 and became *Romanza*. Cruising was to be her fifth, and far longest, career, and she continued with Chandris until 1991. Even at 54 years old, there was deemed to be life in her hull, and she continued operating short cruises in the eastern Mediterranean for new owners as *Romantica*. In 1994 she was reported laid up at Eleusis, but she found new owners once more in 1995, and again

in 1997. The last of these had her only a few months when, on 4th October 1997, a fire broke out in her engine room as she was nearing Limassol on a cruise from Port Said. The passengers and crew were taken off, she was beached and the fire extinguished a few days later. At 60, there was only one possible fate for the ship, and in April 1998 *Romantica* was towed to Alexandria to be demolished. *[Top and bottom: J. and M. Clarkson; middle World Ship Society courtesy G.R. Scott]*

BEAVERFIR

Sarpsborg Mek Verksted, Greaker;
1961, 4,539gt, 374 feet
Oil engine 2SCSA 6-cyl. by
Burmeister & Wain, Copenhagen
The third generation of Beavers
introduced new names, which were
quite appropriate for a country
covered in trees. The first was bought
on the stocks in a Norwegian yard, and
launched as *Beaverfir* in October
1960. In September 1962 she became
the company's first vessel to sail into
the Great Lakes. In a tradition
amongst Great Lakes traders which
has since spread, she carried the
company's name in large letters on
what, in a break from the previous
Beavers, was now a white hull
(above). When repainted in the
colours adopted in 1968, she lost the
name on her hull (below).

Beaverfir was officially the
last ship to carry a Beaver name when
she was sold to flag-of-convenience
owners in 1972. Initially renamed
Arion, after three years she passed to
owners in South America. As
Manaure II she was owned in
Venezuela, and later as *Anden* owned
in Chile and then Peru. In September
1982 she broke her moorings at a port
whose name is reported as Barre de
Santiago, and was wrecked. *[Above: J.*
and M. Clarkson collection; below:
Roy Fenton collection]

BEAVERPINE (top and middle)
Burntisland Shipbuilding Co. Ltd., Burntisland; 1962, 4,514gt, 371 feet 6-cyl. 2SCSA Sulzer-type oil engine made by Fairfield Shipbuilding and Engineering Co. Ltd., Govan.

Following experiments using chartered ice-strengthened ships to serve ports in Quebec all year round, *Beaverpine* was ordered in June 1961. She made her maiden voyage in October 1962, and in the following January became the first Canadian Pacific ship to enter Quebec in winter. Not surprisingly, her master was to win the gold-headed canes awarded by the Quebec ports for the first overseas arrivals each year, awards which the ice-strengthened *Beaverpine* now rendered rather meaningless.

In September 1971 *Beaverpine* was converted to a container ship at the Boele yard in Rotterdam, and was given the corporate name *CP Explorer* in line with the three new building box boats that were emerging from Cammell, Laird's yard (see page 66). Her further service for the company was to be short. Following an agreement with one-time rivals Manchester Liners to share the Canadian business, Canadian Pacific concentrated its services on London and continental ports, withdrawing from Liverpool and Greenock. With fewer ships needed, the slower converted vessels were the obvious ones to sell, and in 1973 *CP Explorer* was sold to become the Liberian flag *Moira*. A further sale in 1981 saw her become the Panama-flagged *Trade Container*, as which she

arrived at Kaohsiung to be broken up at the end of December 1986. *[Top: G.A. Robb, courtesy Peter Newall; middle: World Ship Society, courtesy G.R. Scott]*

BEAVERELM (below and opposite lower)
Moss Vaerft & Dokk A/S, Moss; 1960, 3,964gt, 355 feet
Oil engine 2SCSA 7-cyl. by Burmeister & Wain, Copenhagen
To partially replace the 10,000 ton Beavers built during and just after the war, the company bought the Norwegian *Roga* in August 1962 and sent her for a refit at Hamburg, from which she emerged as *Beaverelm*. A conventional motor ship, she did carry some unusual cargoes, including a French railway locomotive for Montreal and a couple of London buses for Toronto.

With her engines amidships, *Beaverelm* was less suitable than other ships for conversion to carry containers, and so on full containerisation in 1971 she was sold. Buyers were the People's Republic of China, who were at that time disguising their acquisitions by placing them under the ownership of Hong Kong-based front companies. She was initially renamed *Hengshan*, but a 1977 move to place her in the overt ownership of the China Ocean Shipping Co. saw her renamed *Yong Kang*. Like a number of Chinese-owned ships, her fate is a mystery, 'Lloyd's Register' having deleted her for lack of up-to-date information in 1992. *[Opposite: A. Duncan; below: Peter Newall collection]*

BEAVERASH (below)
A/B Ekensbergs Varv., Stockholm; 1958, 4,529gt, 375 feet
Oil engine 2SCSA 7-cyl. by Burmeister & Wain, Copenhagen
Further replacing the older Beavers was the Norwegian *Mimer*, bought in January 1963 and renamed *Beaverash* during an overhaul in Antwerp which saw part of her cargo spaces refrigerated. Of a size with *Beaverelm*, she had engines aft, but she was similar in having a Burmeister & Wain main engine.

Beaverash was the first of the new generation of Beavers to go, in November 1969. Indeed, she may have been surplus to requirements on the St. Lawrence and Great Lakes services as early as September 1968 when she was chartered to T. and J. Harrison for a voyage to the West Indies. From 1969 until she was scrapped at Gadani Beach in 1984 she carried three different names for at least as many Greek owners: *Zanet, Agios Nikolaos* and *Nissaki*. *[World Ship Photo Library]*

BEAVEROAK and CP AMBASSADOR

Vickers Armstrongs Ltd., Walker-on-Tyne, 1965, 408 feet
Clark-Sulzer oil engine 2SCSA 6-cyl. by G. Clark and NEM Ltd., Sunderland.

In anticipation of containerisation, Canadian Pacific ordered *Beaveroak* from the Tyne in January 1964 (top). Her delivery roughly coincided with the sale of the last of the previous generation of Beavers, bringing the owned fleet to five ships.

Highlights of her comparatively short career were carrying the A4-class locomotive 60011 *Dominion of Canada* to the Canadian Historical Railroad Museum at Montreal in 1967, and in 1970 re-opening the service from Greenock, which had been allowed to lapse.

Conversion to a full containership in 1970 took place at the Boelewerft yard in Rotterdam, and also involved lengthening her by 57 feet and renaming her *CP Ambassador:* she is seen right when newly converted. The arrangement with Manchester Liners mentioned above saw the axe fall on this comparatively new ship in 1974, perhaps inevitably as at 15 knots she was a slow-coach compared with the newly-built, 20-knot capable container ships. She was renamed *Atalanta,* but a charter to Zim Israel saw her become *Zim Atalanta* between 1974 and 1980, when after a brief reversion to *Atalanta* she was sold to become *New Penguin* and the next year *Flamingo.* Breaking up at Gadani Beach followed in 1984. *[Top: Roy Fenton collection; right: Gercofoto, Rotterdam, courtesy Peter Newall; below: J. and M. Clarkson]*

THE LIBERTY LINERS
Anthony Cooke

The story of the Liberty ships is, of course, familiar to most of us - although Americans are often innocently unaware that these triumphant examples of their country's expertise in mass production were actually based on a British design. There is, however, one aspect of the Liberty story which is hardly known. Some of these utilitarian freighters were briefly used as passenger liners.

The period immediately following the Second World War witnessed a massive exodus from Europe. It is hard now to realise just how grim life was then. The 1939-1945 War had devastated large parts of the continent. Food, coal, raw materials - almost everything was in short supply and, to make matters worse, the winter of 1946-47 was one of the harshest on record. There were political problems, too. Almost inexorably, the Communists were taking over, as the nations of eastern Europe fell, one by one, under the domination of Soviet Russia - with Greece and Italy in real danger of being the next to go. Another problem was posed by the refugees who either huddled discontentedly in camps or roamed in bands across the continent. It was estimated that there were fourteen million of them in Europe, categorised as 'displaced persons'. Perhaps a million of them would have to be settled overseas - in the United States, Canada, Venezuela, the Argentine, Australia, New Zealand and elsewhere. The International Refugee Organisation, a Geneva-based offshoot of the United Nations, therefore drew up a Mass Resettlement Plan.

Refugees were not the only migrants. Thousands of others, often newly returned servicemen, decided that they and their families deserved something better than Europe could apparently offer. There was, for instance, a huge exodus from Italy, inflated by the urgent desire to leave of some who had become politically compromised during the Mussolini years.

Passenger ships needed
Before the age of the jet airliner, all this required a vast number of passenger ships. But where were they to be found? Roughly one half of the pre-war passenger fleet had either been destroyed or was no longer available for civilian service. True, the Americans made a number of their troopships available but more bottoms were urgently needed. Some highly entrepreneurial shipowners saw this as a great opportunity. Many of them had been involved in the freight trades before the war and often they were either Italian or Italian-based. Such owners as the Costa family; Alexandre Vlasov of the Sitmar Line; Evgen Evgenides of the Home Lines; Achille Lauro; his nephews, the Grimaldi brothers; and Ignazio Messina scoured the World for ships, however old and apparently unsuitable, which could be converted to carry human cargo. There were some astonishing transformations: the Greek Yannoulatos family, for instance, turned a former Royal Australian Navy seaplane tender into a grotesque-looking emigrant ship, the *Hellenic Prince*. Achille Lauro conjured the passenger liners *Ravello* and *Napoli* out of the wrecks of two sunken freighters. Several firms used quite elaborately converted Victory ships in emigrant service. 'Baby flat-tops', aircraft carriers which were based on American C3-type merchant ship hulls, were also converted. All this is well-known, but what has been almost forgotten is that some Liberty ships were also used to carry passengers.

The Liberty ship was a 7,000-ton, five-hold freighter with an overall length of 441 feet 6 inches. An old-fashioned triple-expansion steam engine, fed by two oil-fired boilers, drove a single screw. A service speed of just 11 knots was usually quoted. These were very basic, very simple ships, designed to be mass produced quickly and in huge quantities during the Second World War. Built to carry supplies to the Allied forces around the world, they were welded together from pre-fabricated sections in specially-constructed yards strung along the American coasts. The famous journalist Alistair Cooke visited one of these facilities and commented that it was 'like a giant, numbered chessboard'. On one specially-staged occasion, a publicity stunt intended to encourage the sale of War Bonds, a Liberty ship was launched just 4 days 15½ hours after her keel had been laid. Amazingly, her total construction time was no more than 8 days. In all, no fewer than 2,710 Liberty ships were built between 1941 and 1945, including a number which were of modified tanker or collier design. It was accepted that many of them would inevitably be lost by enemy action.

Hellenic Prince, a former Australian seaplane carrier, seen at a South Wales port shortly after her conversion.
[Laurence Dunn]

Human cargoes

The idea of using them to carry human cargo was taken up during the war. It is thought that over 30 were converted into troopships. They carried up to about 500 'passengers' in tiered berths which, together with the other necessary facilities, were crammed into the 'tween decks. Much more fundamental alterations were made to a further six Liberties, which, in 1943-1944, were converted into hospital ships for the US Army. In each case, the hull was still recognisably that of a Liberty but it was now topped by a long, two deck-high superstructure and a shortish, raked funnel. The regulation red crosses were painted on the funnel and the sides of the hull.

The Liberties which, in the post-war years, were used by opportunist private owners to carry passengers were not nearly so obviously altered. Indeed, most of them were probably never regarded as anything more than very temporary, stopgap passenger ships which could be easily returned to their original cargo-carrying rôle once the emigrant boom was over. It is difficult to establish now just how many Liberties were employed in this way, but I have listed below all those which have come to my notice.

Olimpia

This was the best-known of the 'Liberty liners'. She had been built for the US Navy in 1943 by the St. Johns River Shipbuilding Corporation of Jacksonville, Florida and had a gross tonnage of 7,240. She was then called *Shaula* but, when transferred to the War Shipping Administration and laid up in 1946, she was renamed *James Screven*. In 1947, she was one of the 95 Liberties which the American administration allotted to the Italians. The government in Rome passed her in turn to the formidable Neapolitan shipowner and right-wing politician, Achille Lauro, who gave her the name *Olimpia*. She left Seattle on the 6th August 1947 and after three transatlantic crossings, freighter voyages of the kind that dozens of other Liberties were making at the time, she arrived in Genoa on the 15th November. There, she was taken in hand for conversion into a passenger carrier. The enterprising Lauro was beginning a semi-regular service from Italy to the east coast of South America and, like several other owners, decided to cater for

migrant passengers as well as cargo. Cabin accommodation was fitted for 48 passengers in what was designated first class, although it is hard to imagine that this denoted much in the way of luxury. More humble and more numerous were the 430 passengers whom she carried in dormitories, almost certainly crowded into the 'tween decks which were equipped with collapsible berths. The ship's appearance was changed by several outcrops of new deckhousing and by 14 lifeboats, rather than the four which Liberties usually carried.

With much of her accommodation block-booked to the International Refugee Organisation, the *Olimpia* left Genoa on the 29th January 1948 and, after a brief call at Tenerife, headed for Rio de Janeiro, Santos, Montevideo, Buenos Aires and Rosario. As had been the case with generations of emigrant ships, the 'tween deck accommodation was probably dismantled before she embarked on the return voyage, so as to make room for extra cargo. The holds would almost certainly be filled with much-needed Argentine grain. The *Olimpia* made eleven of these round trips from Genoa, often picking up passengers at other Italian ports and, on a couple of occasions, having reached Buenos Aires, she went further south to Bahia Blanca.

By 1951, however, the Argentine economy was no longer booming and the country had ceased to be a magnet for migrants. (Only a few years earlier, the Peron regime had agreed with the governments in Rome and Madrid that several million Italians and Spaniards should come to the Argentine.) Some shipowners withdrew from the trade, including Achille Lauro who was, in any case, developing a new passenger service to Australia. He also entered what was generally called the Central American trade, although in fact most ships sailed to the Caribbean islands and Venezuela rather than to the Central American republics. The *Olimpia* was transferred to this route, running to Curaçao and to La Guaira. Large numbers of Italians were now emigrating to Venezuela but it is not certain whether the *Olimpia* continued to carry passengers. Lauro had other, more suitable liners coming onto the route and the new SOLAS (Safety of Life at Sea) regulations, drawn up at a conference in London in 1948, were due to come fully into

Achille Lauro's *Olimpia*. [A. Bisagno]

force in November 1952. It would be expensive to modify this stopgap Liberty liner to comply with the new rules and, since she had a speed of only 11 knots, would it be worth it?

However, she continued in the Lauro fleet, running not only to Venezuela but to many other parts of the World. In the mid-1950s, she went through a rather eventful phase, experiencing several groundings and collisions. It was not, however, until October, 1968 that she was withdrawn and sold to shipbreakers at La Spezia.

Lauro had other Liberty ships: the *Aida Lauro* (ex-*John Einig*), the *Angelina Lauro* (ex-*Benjamin H. Brewster*), the *Gioacchino Lauro* (ex-*Luther S. Kelly*) and the *Laura Lauro* (ex-*Elwood Haynes*). Unlike the *Olimpia*, they were never equipped to carry large numbers of passengers but it is known that at least two, the *Gioacchino Lauro* and the *Laura Lauro*, did carry small contingents of migrants on occasion. They were both of 7,176 tons and had been built at the Permanente Metals Corporation yard No. 2 at Richmond, California in 1943 and 1944 respectively.

Francesco Barbaro

Another firm which was early into the post-war migrant business was 'Sidarma' - one of those acronymic Italian company names, in this case standing for Società Italiana d'Armamento. 'Sidarma' was based in Venice. It had entered the tramping trades just before the War but now also became a vigorous competitor in the passenger business on the routes to the Argentine and to Venezuela, mainly using two modern motor vessels which had originally been designed as freighters. At times, however, 'Sidarma' also pressed Liberties into passenger service. The first, *Francesco Barbaro*, was, like several 'Sidarma' ships, named after a famous Doge of Venice. She had been the *Alfred C. True* (7,176 gross tons, Permanente Metals Corporation Yard No. 2, 1944) and she carried passengers on a few voyages to Buenos Aires in 1947 and 1948, while the company was awaiting the delivery of the new motor ship *Francesco Morosini*. She also saw North Atlantic service, making voyages to Hampton Roads, presumably for cargo only, and it was during one of these, in December 1947, that she lost her propeller (a common mishap with Liberties) and damaged her rudder. She did not last long in the 'Sidarma' fleet, being sold in 1949.

Laguna

Also in 1949, however, the company added another Liberty to their fleet, the *Jesse Billingsley*, which had been damaged by a mine in the Adriatic three years previously. 'Sidarma' were enthusiasts for the motor ship and they not only had their new purchase repaired but they also installed a six-cylinder FIAT diesel engine, thus slightly increasing her speed. She had been built in 1943 by the Houston Shipbuilding Corporation and had a gross tonnage of 7,215. 'Sidarma' registered her as the *Laguna* for some years in the name of an associated company which had revived the historic title of Navigazione Libera Triestina. Advertisements offered accommodation on her South American voyages and she was reported to have been fitted with berths for 100 passengers, while still remaining primarily a cargo-carrier. It is difficult to know how long she continued to carry passengers. After 1951, the voyage records shew that she was mainly running across the North Atlantic, visiting such ports as New York, Albany, Philadelphia, Hampton Roads and Baltimore. In any case, 'Sidarma' withdrew from the passenger business in about 1955. The *Laguna* passed through the hands of two other Italian shipowners before being scrapped in Spain in 1969 after suffering an engine breakdown and leaks in her hull. In addition to the *Laguna*, 'Sidarma' acquired a second mine-damaged Liberty and converted her to diesel propulsion. The *Abbott L. Mills* became their *Corallo* and she too was registered in the name of Navigazione Libera Triestina. Whether she ever saw any passenger service is not clear.

'Sidarma' also formed an alliance with 'Italnavi' Società di Navigazione per Azioni of Genoa, a company associated with the FIAT group, and the two lines co-ordinated their services. 'Italnavi' also installed FIAT diesels in a pair of Liberties, the *Walter Wyman,* which became their *Italcielo,* and the *Henry V. Alvarado,* which they renamed *Italmare.* Again, it is not known whether they were given any passenger accommodation.

Emanuele V. Parodi

At one time it seemed that another Italian Liberty, the *Emanuele V. Parodi,* would also carry passengers. In 1947 it was announced that she would offer passages from Genoa to New York at $300 per person, a rate which would seem to indicate that she was to be fitted with cabin accommodation. In the event, apart from her delivery voyage from New York to Genoa, she did not operate on this route, mainly voyaging instead between Genoa and Baltimore.

The Parodi were an old-established Genovese shipping family and that year they had been allotted two Liberties, the aforementioned *Emanuele V. Parodi* (7,176 gross tons, built in 1944 at the Permanente Metals Corporation shipyard No. 1 at Richmond, California as the *Joseph E. Wing*) and the *Maria Parodi* (ex-*William I. Chamberlain*, 7,176 gross tons, Oregon Shipbuilding Corporation, Portland, 1944). Again, whether or not the *Maria Parodi* ever carried passengers is not known. The family company, SpA Emanuele V. Parodi, bought a further three Liberties from other owners in 1949 and 1950 and named them *Angelo Parodi, Elena Parodi* and *Isa Parodi* but by then any interest they had in the passenger trade had almost certainly faded.

Andrea

The Parodi family were also involved in two other Genovese shipping firms, Società di Navigazione 'Polena' and Società Anonima di Navigazione 'Corrado'. Both owned Liberties and one at least, Corrado's *Andrea* (ex-*Robert Trimble*, 7,176 gross tons, J. A. Jones Construction Co. of Brunswick, Georgia, 1943), may have carried passengers on voyages from Genoa and Savona to Philadelphia and to Baltimore in the period 1947-1949.

Etna, Nereide, Stròmboli and Vesuvio

Whatever the doubts about the Parodi group's involvement in the passenger trades, it is certain that Italia SpA di Navigazione did use Liberties in regular passenger service. Famously known outside its home country as the Italian Line, Italia was one of the four big, state-owned shipping companies, to each of which the Mussolini government had allotted its own sphere of influence in the 1930s. Italia was given charge of the services across the North and South Atlantic. After the war, such was the devastation which had been wrought on the Italian merchant marine that it was some years before it was possible for the company to resume full-scale passenger sailings from the Adriatic ports of Trieste and Venice. The prime routes from Genoa and Naples had to take priority. Nevertheless, cargo services were re-established from the Adriatic and among the ships used on these routes were four of the five Liberties which the line was allotted in 1946 and 1947.

Three of them were named after volcanoes: *Etna* (ex-*Juan Pablo Duarte*, 7,212 gross tons, Permanente Metals Corporation yard No. 2, 1944), *Stròmboli* (ex-*Morgan Robertson*, 7,176 gross tons, Permanente Metals

Nereide at the end of her career at Vado in 1973, with little external evidence that she had ever carried passengers. *[Paolo Piccione collection]*

Stromboli. [Eric Johnson, courtesy Peter Newall]

Vesuvio, another of Italia's Liberties. *[Peter Newall collection]*

Corporation yard No. 2, 1944) and *Vesuvio* (ex-*William P. Duval*, 7,176 gross tons, J. A. Jones Construction Co., Panama City, Florida, 1944). The fourth was called *Nereide* (ex-*Norman Hapgood*, 7,176 gross tons, Permanente Metals Corporation yard No. 2, 1943). Initially, they were mainly used on the route to the east coast of South America. A Spanish source shews that, on a number of their calls at Santa Cruz de Tenerife during 1948 and 1949, they were carrying about 50 passengers en route for Buenos Aires. In the case of the *Nereide*, it is recorded that she had accommodation for 24 tourist class (i.e. cabin) passengers and 32 who bedded down in dormitories. Her return to service was delayed by damage she sustained when she struck a mine. Eventually, the four Liberties were able to maintain a monthly passenger/cargo service on the Trieste - Buenos Aires route. Unlike her sisters, the *Stròmboli* carried 12 passengers only.

In 1949, the Liberties helped to revive the pre-war service from both coasts of Italy to the West Coast of America (Los Angeles, San Francisco, Portland, Seattle, Tacoma, Vancouver). In this they were joined by the line's other Liberty, the *Tritone* (ex-*Alexander Majors*, 7,176 gross tons, Permanente Metals Corporation yard No. 1, 1944, fitted to carry 12 passengers) and by an elderly combination liner, the *Leme*. This was mainly a cargo service, but the *Leme* could carry up to 322 passengers and the Liberties retained their limited accommodation. But it was a very long route with numerous calls for cargo; and all the ships had a service speed of no more than

11 knots. It was hardly an express run, therefore, and, in any case, passenger numbers were always likely to be small. Nevertheless, the Italian Line did its best to sell the service. An English-language brochure with the title 'Half A World On One Voyage' (right) dangled this blandishment: 'This itinerary affords a voyage full of variety, rich in interest, one calculated to restore one's flagging energies after the feverish tempo of modern life. Man's primitive, undying sense of great distances revives during this voyage over the boundless ocean, and the colourful succession of far away ports brings home to one the mysterious fascination of unknown countries and gives one an almost Homeric sense of adventure.'

The Liberties continued as the mainstays of the service until 1956-57, when that rôle was assumed by three superior vessels which Italia had bought from Chargeurs Réunis - much to the fury of the French government, who henceforth exercised a very strict control over the sale of important French ships. Italia now stripped the Liberties of their passenger quarters and employed them in cargo service until selling them for scrap in 1962 (*Etna*) and 1973 (the others).

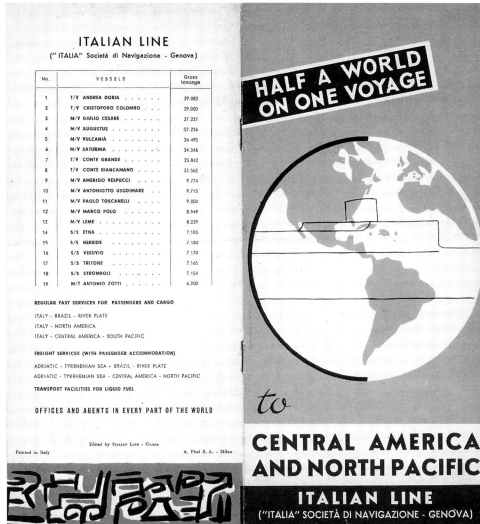

ITALIAN LINE
("ITALIA" Società di Navigazione - Genova)

No.	VESSELS	Gross tonnage
1	T/V ANDREA DORIA	29.083
2	T/V CRISTOFORO COLOMBO	29.000
3	M/V GIULIO CESARE	27.227
4	M/V AUGUSTUS	27.226
5	M/V VULCANIA	24.495
6	M/V SATURNIA	24.346
7	T/V CONTE GRANDE	23.842
8	T/V CONTE BIANCAMANO	23.562
9	M/V AMERIGO VESPUCCI	9.774
10	M/V ANTONIOTTO USODIMARE	9.715
11	M/V PAOLO TOSCANELLI	9.004
12	M/V MARCO POLO	8.949
13	M/V LEME	8.039
14	S/S ETNA	7.183
15	S/S NEREIDE	7.180
16	S/S VESUVIO	7.170
17	S/S TRITONE	7.165
18	S/S STROMBOLI	7.154
19	M/T ANTONIO ZOTTI	6.200

REGULAR FAST SERVICES FOR PASSENGERS AND CARGO

ITALY - BRAZIL - RIVER PLATE
ITALY - NORTH AMERICA
ITALY - CENTRAL AMERICA - SOUTH PACIFIC

FREIGHT SERVICES (WITH PASSENGER ACCOMMODATION)

ADRIATIC - TYRRHENIAN SEA - BRAZIL - RIVER PLATE
ADRIATIC - TYRRHENIAN SEA - CENTRAL AMERICA - NORTH PACIFIC

TRANSPORT FACILITIES FOR LIQUID FUEL

OFFICES AND AGENTS IN EVERY PART OF THE WORLD

Printed in Italy   Edited by ITALIAN LINE - Genoa   A. Pizzi S. A. - Milan

HALF A WORLD ON ONE VOYAGE

to

CENTRAL AMERICA AND NORTH PACIFIC

ITALIAN LINE
("ITALIA" SOCIETÀ DI NAVIGAZIONE - GENOVA)

Enrico C. and Eugenio C.

The Genovese firm of Giacomo Costa, fu Andrea (i.e.: Giacomo, successor of Andrea Costa) also used Liberties to supplement their regular passenger sailings for a time. Before the Second World War, the Costa family had owned a fleet of small freighters which they had used mainly to bring supplies to their olive oil refinery at Sampierdarena in Genoa. Now they had much grander ambitions and started services to North and South America. In 1946-47,

they acquired their first two Liberties: the *Frank H. Evers* (7,176 gross tons, Permanente Metals Corporation yard No. 2, 1943), which they renamed *Enrico C.*; and the *Edwin G. Weed* (7,240 gross tons, St. Johns River Shipbuilding Corporation, 1944), which became the *Eugenio C.* There is no doubt that these ships carried passengers for a while - as the accompanying photographs, provided by Paolo Piccione, demonstrate. A third Liberty, the *Federico Costa*, was not bought by Costa until 1952 and was presumably too late to join her sisters in passenger service. The three ships remained in the Costa fleet until 1963, 1963 and 1960 respectively, all being sold for further service.

The Genovese *Enrico C.* [Peter Newall collection]

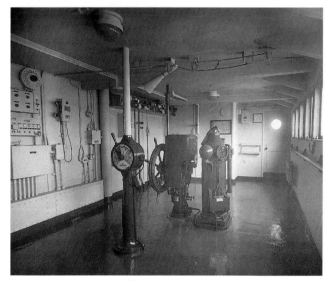

Top: *Eugenio C* on 13th January 1952; lower left a three-berth cabin; lower right her wheelhouse. *[Top: G.A. Osbon, courtesy Peter Newall; lower: both Paolo Piccione]*

Andrea C., the converted 'Ocean'

Another Costa purchase, the *Andrea C.*, was not actually a Liberty ship, but she was a close cousin of those famous vessels. She had a very long and very successful career as a genuine passenger liner and cruise ship and deserves to be mentioned in this article. She was, in fact, an Ocean-class ship, one of the vessels which the British government ordered from North American builders in the early days of the Second World War.

Desperate for replacements for the terrible losses which the British merchant fleet was suffering, they contracted with Canadian yards to build a series of standard ships which became known as the Forts and the Parks. American builders were also approached and it was the prospect of a huge contract for vessels which could be mass-produced which attracted Henry J. Kaiser, an entrepreneur with a flair for big projects. His companies had built huge dams and other civil engineering works as part of President Franklin Delano Roosevelt's New Deal programme, which in the late thirties helped to drag the United States out of the Great Depression. Now, although he had no previous experience of shipbuilding, Kaiser constructed yards especially to assemble ships for the British. The Ocean class, as they were called, were produced to a design from the Joseph L. Thompson and Sons shipyard of Sunderland. In modified form, this was eventually adopted as the basis for the US government's Liberty ship programme.

The ship which later became the *Andrea C.* was built in 1942 at one of the Kaiser-controlled facilities, Permanente Metals Corporation shipyard No.1 at Richmond, near San Francisco. She was called *Ocean Virtue* and was placed under the management of the Prince Line. Sunk by a German aerial torpedo in July 1943, while lying in the port of Augusta following the Allied invasion of Sicily, she was raised and laid up. In 1946, she was bought by Giacomo Costa fu Andrea.

The *Ocean Virtue* was to be one of the Linea Costa's South American ships and, under the name *Andrea C.*, would carry large numbers of passengers as well as cargo. Her conversion by the Cantieri del Tirreno of Genoa was said to be the first case of a Second World War standard ship being turned into a fully-fledged commercial passenger liner. Her coal-fired furnaces and her steam engine were replaced by a wartime 8-cylinder FIAT diesel and a long, low superstructure was spread along the after two thirds of the hull, surmounted by a low, motor-ship funnel. Now with a gross tonnage of 7,800, she had comfortable cabin accommodation for 79 first class passengers, who enjoyed the use of a swimming pool and lido, while a further 384 could be housed in third class dormitories in the 'tween decks.

The *Andrea C.* departed Genoa on her maiden voyage to Santos, Montevideo and Buenos Aires on the 27th June 1948. Between 1948 and 1959, she made 62 round voyages on this route and also, after 1952, a number of cruises.

Two views of the *Andrea C,* unrecognisable as the former *Ocean Virtue. [Peter Newall collection]*

By 1959, the Linea Costa had become one of the major competitors on the South and Central American routes, with a fleet of high-class liners. If the *Andrea C.* was to remain a Costa ship, she must be upgraded to the standards of her fleet mates. A new and more powerful FIAT Grandi Motori diesel engine was installed and her appearance was modernised. She was given a longer, more raked bow; her superstructure was extended; and a larger funnel was fitted. Internally, she was almost completely revamped and, with some of her former cargo space now filled with cabins, she could carry 122 first class passengers and 354 in tourist class. Dormitory accommodation was a thing of the past. While still making line voyages, the *Andrea C.* was increasingly used for cruises, both from South American ports (including voyages up the Amazon) and in the Mediterranean.

A further refit in 1970 transformed her still further. She was now fully air-conditioned; every cabin had private facilities; her public rooms were remodelled. She could now carry 464 passengers in a single class and was quite unrecognisable as the hastily built standard-type freighter which had left the builders' yard in 1943. Virtually a full-time cruise ship, she became extremely popular, both with Italian and South American passengers. For a few years, some of her cruises were marketed in Britain by Saga Holidays. She lasted until the end of her 1981 season, when she was laid up. The following year, this hardy veteran was sold to another Italian operator who needed an old ship in order to attract a Scrap and Build subsidy for a new one. She was broken up at La Spezia in 1982.

An oriental mystery

In the 1960s, by which time the numbers of Liberties were beginning to thin, there were reports from the Far East of sightings of an example which had been given an extended superstructure and an unusually large number of lifeboats. The assumption was that she was a passenger carrier and that she was Chinese. Nobody seemed able to give her a name, but this was not entirely surprising since western observers often find the characters painted on the bows and sterns of Chinese vessels almost impenetrable.

Very strangely, it is possible that this mystery ship made one voyage under the name *Ignacy Krasicki,* with a Polish crew and flying the Polish flag. According to Bohdan Huras, the authority on Polish merchant shipping, a Chinese Liberty was handed over to the Poles for a single voyage from Canton to Shanghai in September 1962. The object of the arrangement was apparently to avoid the risk of her being seized by the Taiwanese navy while she was en route. It is difficult to establish which ship she was, but Bohdan Huras thinks she may have been the former *John W. Weeks* (7,176 gross tons, built in 1943 by the Oregon Ship Building Corporation, Portland). She had been taken over by the US Navy and converted into the self-propelled barracks ship *Du Page* - hence the obvious addition of passenger capacity. In 1959, she was stricken from the list and offered for sale. What happened to her after that is shrouded in mystery but she would seem eventually to have found her way into Chinese hands. On arrival in Canton she was renamed *Zhong Hua.* She did not appear in *Lloyd's Register,* however.

It will be seen that the story of the Liberty liners is full of interesting uncertainties. As far as I am aware, the ships noted above are a complete list of the Liberties (plus an Ocean) which were pressed into passenger service. It may be, however, that there were others. If any readers have further information on this somewhat obscure episode in post-war shipping history, I shall be delighted to hear from them.

FURTHER FINNS IN THE FIFTIES

An interesting selection of photographs of Finnish steamers mostly from the fifties kindly supplied by Alex Duncan persuaded the editors that we would reopen the file on these ships, closed - we thought - after the feature in *Record* 23. All photos are Alex's unless indicated.

Lakers

Two unusual-looking Finns, both photographed at Cape Town, turn out to have been veterans built for service on the canals feeding the Great Lakes. They were a special breed - general cargo ships, which are referred to as package freighters on the Lakes. Cargo was mainly handled through sideports and internal elevators. Prior to the completion of the enlarged Welland Canal around 1934, they were confined to Lake Erie and to Lake Superior, and after that could have sailed no further than Cornwall, Ontario and Ogdensburg, New York. To help meet the urgent demand for ocean-going tonnage during the Second World War they were stripped to the main deck and taken out of the Lakes via the Chicago Ship and Sanitary Canal and the Illinois River to the Mississippi. Interestingly, both were fitted with quadruple-expansion steam engines, relatively rare on ocean-going ships of their size.

KURIKKA (below)

Union Dry Dock Company, Buffalo, N.Y.; 1899/1943, 4,404g, 392 feet
Q. 4-cyl. by the Cleveland Ship-building Company, Cleveland, Ohio
Named after the base of both her owners, the Western Transit Co, and her builders, the *Buffalo* became *P.E. Crowley* in 1925, but her big adventure was to become a proper deep-sea ship after the United States War Shipping Administration bought her in 1942 and sent her off for a rebuild by Dixie Marine Welding & Metal Works, New Orleans. On sale to Finland in 1947 she became *Kurikka* of Kurikan Laiva O/Y, managed by Paul Eriksson of Vasa. Seen here in December 1951, the 52-year old hull and engine had only a little more life in them, and arrived at Briton Ferry for scrapping by T.W. Ward Ltd. in April 1953.

PANKAKOSKI (below)

Detroit Shipbuilding Company, Wyandotte, Michigan; 1909/1943, 4,138gt, 362 feet
Q. 4-cyl. by Detroit Shipbuilding Company, Wyandotte, Michigan
Although built for different owners, this ship had a parallel career to *Kurikka*. Original owners were Erie and Western Transportation Company, Erie, Pennsylvania who named her *Conemaugh*. Passing like *Kurikka* to Great Lakes Transit Corporation, Buffalo during the First World War, she was later renamed *W.W. Atterbury*. The US War Shipping Administration had her rebuilt by Todd-Johnson Drydocks, Algiers, Lousiana: note the similarity of her mast to those on *Kurikka*. In 1947 *W.W. Atterbury* returned briefly to US civilian ownership, with Overlakes Freight Corporation of Detroit. In 1948, she became the *Pankakoski* of O/Y Merivienti (O/Y Baltic Chartering A/B), Helsingfors. She was in her last months when photographed in July 1953, as in December 1953 she arrived at Hong King to be broken up by Lunghua Dock and Engineering Works Co. Ltd.

Ex-German

ALBERTINA (above)
Flensburger Schiffsbau Ges., Flensburg; 1913, 5,930gt, 450 feet
T.3-cyl. by Flensburger Schiffsbau Ges., Flensburg
This ship had the misfortune to be twice taken from the Germans as war reparations. Built as *Cannstatt* for Deutsch-Australische D.G., Hamburg, she was in Brisbane when war broke out in August 1914 and was immediately seized by the Australians,

and renamed *Bakara*. As so many ex-German ships did, she found her way back to German ownership between the wars, becoming *Witell* of Roland Linie, Bremen. By the outbreak of the next war, she was the *Rosario* of Hamburg-Südamerika D.G. and was heavily damaged in an air raid in her home port of Hamburg in April 1945. After the war she was allocated to Denmark, but appears never to have run for this country, but was repaired and sold to Finland as *Albertina* with owners Pargas Rederi & Varvs A/B

(O/Y Northern Chartering), Helsingfors. This photograph at Cape Town during December 1948 must have been taken within a few months of her entering Finnish service. In 1950 she was sold to other Finnish owners and renamed *Kotka*. Her end is a little sinister. Sold in 1956 to the British Ministry of Transport, she was scuttled in Mid-Atlantic with condemned ammunition. Was this poison gas, and if so why was it disposed of so long after the war?

Another ship called *Wanda*

WANDA
Helsingørs Jernskibsvft. & Maskinbyg., Helsingør; 1897, 1,918gt, 290 feet.
T. 3-cyl. by Helsingørs Jernskibsvft. &

Maskinbyg., Helsingør
This ship was the immediate predecessor in the fleet of A/B Baltic Lloyd Line Ltd. O/Y (H. Janhonen, manager), Helsinki of the *Wanda* depicted on page 174 of *Record* 23. The *Wanda* shown here was built as

Skanderborg for the well-known Copenhagen shipowner C. K. Hansen and sold and renamed *Wanda* in 1933. In 1955 she was replaced in Janhonen's fleet and became the *Ridal* for other Finnish owners. She was broken up at Grimstad in 1958.

Ex-British

HERAKLES (top)
Russell and Co., Port Glasgow; 1910, 5,047gt, 423 feet
T. 3-cyl. by David Rowan and Co., Glasgow

Herakles provides a link with a fleet of sailing ships owned by Gillison and Chadwick, featured way back in *Record 9*.

She was built as *Drumcraig* for the Astral Shipping Co. Ltd. managed by Joseph Chadwick and Sons, who were the successors of Gillison and Chadwick and inherited their *Drum-* names. *Drumcraig* had the honour of being the first Liverpool ship to carry wireless, but was soon sold. In 1913 she became the *Vinstra* of Dampsk. Den Norske Afrika og Australielinje, a venture managed jointly by Norwegians Wilhelm Wilhelmsen and Fearnley & Eger. In 1920 Wilhelmsen became sole managers and in 1934 nominal owner, but *Vinstra* did not take one of his 'T' names.

Finnish ownership began in

1936, with her becoming *Herakles* for A/B Oceanfart (Birger Krogius, manager), Helsinki. In 1950 Curt Mattson also of Helsinki acquired *Herakles*, which was in his ownership when she was photographed off Tilbury in 1953. She was broken up at Hong Kong by Mollers Ltd. in 1958.

SALLY (middle)
William Gray and Co. Ltd., West Hartlepool, 1896, 2,547gt, 325 feet
T. 3-cyl. by Central Marine Engine Works, West Hartlepool

Algot Johansson of Mariehamn had a substantial fleet of tramps in the 1950s, some owned by A/B Sally, a name which became better known when he formed Sally Ferries. His motorship *Dafny* was featured in *Record 23*, but here is a steamer from his fleet. Original owners were R. Hardy and Co. of West Hartlepools, for whom she was built locally as *Greylands*. In 1899 she was sold to France as *Edmond-Gustave* and had the misfortune to be caught in the

Baltic at the outbreak of the First World War. Sale to Swedish owners was arranged in 1916, and she became *Norrköping,* one of the select band of ships to be named after her homeport, so her stern read *Norrköping, Norrköping.* She was later named *Oswal* by other Swedish owners. Algot Johansson bought her in 1937 and gave her the name *Sally.* Some idea of her wartime employment is gained from her being mined on 11th May 1940, not far from Helsingør, Denmark whilst on a voyage from Göteborg to Memel in ballast. The British had probably laid this mine as part of their effort to restrict shipments of Swedish iron ore to Germany. *Sally* was beached and later refloated for repairs.

Sally was photographed in Surrey Commercial Docks in January 1953 during what must have been her last cargo-carrying voyage. On 30th January 1953, she arrived at Hamburg having been sold to Metall-Union, Reed. Heinrich Flugger who began demolishing her in March.

ELLEN (bottom)
William Gray and Co., West Hartlepool; 1878, 1,597gt, 266 feet
C. 2-cyl. by T. Richardson and Sons, Hartlepool

Definitely the grandmother of the ships in this feature, *Ellen* was a very respectable 75 years old when photographed in Surrey Commercial Docks in 1953. That she does not look her age must be put down to a radical reconstruction at some time, although 'Lloyd's Register' is silent on when and where this took place.

She was originally *Hathersage,* owned in West Hartlepool by J. Merryweather and Co. She was sold by them in 1897, becoming *Ellen* for Swedish owners. She was sold to Finland in 1938, and by the time she was photographed was owned by Rederi A/B Ellen, and managed by H. Liljestrand O/Y A/B of Rauma. Believing there was more mileage in her old iron hull, these owners renamed her *Harriet* in 1954.

Tough her hull may have been, but conditions in the Baltic in the spring of 1957 were too much for her, and on 20th March 1957 she grounded at the entrance to Hango with all her holds flooded due to ice damage. She was declared a total loss, but refloated so that her cargo could be discharged in Hango harbour, and from there went to Hamburg where she arrived in June to be demolished.

VELI RAGNAR (above)
Craig, Taylor and Co., Ltd., Stockton;
1914, 2,185gt, 287 feet
T. 3-cyl. by North Eastern Marine
Engineering Co. Ltd., Sunderland
Although later much better known for their coastal tramps, owned by the Kyle Shipping Co. Ltd. of Liverpool, the Monroe family started in shipowning at Cardiff with bigger ships. The partnership Monroe, Rutherford and Co. Ltd., managed the Underwood Shipping Co. Ltd., of which the second and last vessel, and its only newbuilding, was the *Banchory* of 1914. With prices escalating with the loss of so much tonnage, *Banchory* was sold to other Cardiff owners in 1917. She survived the conflict and indeed retained her name until sold to Swedish owners in 1931, when she became *Torgny Lagman*. In 1938 she went to her final owner, Lovisa Rederi A/B, managed by A/B R. Nordström & Co. O/Y, Lovisa who we met in the early feature on Finns. *Veli Ragnar*, as she became, is seen here in July 1955, probably on the River Medway. She was broken up at Hamburg in 1958. *[World Ship Photo Library]*

Finns in the thirties
Stretching our time frame, we include two veteran Finns which did not survive the Second World War.

NAXOS (middle)
Charles Connell and Co. Ltd., Glasgow; 1897, 4,157gt, 377 feet T. 3-cyl. by Dunsmuir and Jackson, Glasgow
Scottish shipowners found it hard to resist names of glens, and there are several examples other than the celebrated Glen Line: for instance, J. Gardner and Co. used the name

Glenaffric for this steamer. Furness, Withy and Co. Ltd. bought her in 1917 but only in 1922 bestowing the name *Saxon Prince*. This was only carried until 1924, when she was sold to A/B Naxos Prince managed by R. Mattson of Helsinki and renamed *Naxos,* as seen here. Perhaps surprisingly, she found a further owner, this time in Genoa, who renamed her *Ogaden* in 1936. She was torpedoed by the British submarine *Porpoise* on 12th August 1942 whilst taking supplies into Tobruk.

WIIRI (bottom)
Craig, Taylor and Co., Ltd., Stockton; 1912, 3,525gt, 361 feet T. 3-cyl. by North Eastern Marine Engineering Co. Ltd., Sunderland
Wiiri was one of the relatively few Finnish ships that served the Allied cause. She was bombed and sunk in

the Mediterranean on 17th July 1940 whilst carrying coal from the Tyne to Piraeus. Less than a year later, in June 1941, Finland joined with Germany and other Axis powers in invading the USSR which led to Finland being declared an enemy by Britain.

The ship had already changed hands because of one war, her original owners - Dampfschiffs Rhederei 'Horn' A.G. of Lübeck - losing her as *Hornfels* in 1919 when she was handed over to Britain as reparations. A variety of mainly South Welsh owners then had her, no doubt using her in the Bay and Mediterranean coal trades. She ran first as *Tempestuous*, then as *Northway* and lastly as *Charterhulme*, before being sold to Finland in 1931. As *Wiiri* she was owned from 1931 until her loss by Wiiri O/Y with Antti Wihuri of Helsinki as manager.

THE INNIS BOATS: A REAPPRAISAL
Roy Fenton

In 1912 Glasgow shipowner John M. Paton formed the Coasting Motor Shipping Co. Ltd. to build and operate the first substantial fleet of motor vessels to run in the British, or probably any other, coastal trade. He ordered no fewer than 18 small vessels, varying in size from 66 to 115 feet, from four builders, and equipped with four different types of oil engine. All were given names prefixed 'Innis'. Not unexpectedly with a pioneering venture on this scale, there were problems, both mechanical and human, and the fleet was dispersed during and soon after the First World War. The venture has been routinely dismissed as a failure[1] but, with several of the 'Innis' boats surviving to ripe old ages, the author feels this was too hasty a judgement. This article aims to make a reappraisal of the fleet of Coasting Motor Shipping by looking at the individual ships and their careers. Although the analysis and opinions are the author's, the article could not have been compiled without help, especially from David Burrell who kindly supplied much information and read through a draft, and others mentioned in the acknowledgements.

The first shipowning venture traced for John Muir Paton is the wooden steamer *Major* (156/1874) in which he acquired an interest in 1888. His career gathered momentum in 1892 when he formed a partnership with Peter D. Hendry which rapidly built up a fleet of small and medium sized-coasters, many of which were registered in the ownership of the Glasgow Steam Coasters Co. Ltd. A total of 37 vessels were listed in 'Lloyd's Registers' under the partners' ownership or management during the next 20 years, but contemporary 'Mercantile Navy Lists' show there were a number of further vessels under 100 tons, and the total was probably around 50. In 1911 Paton left the partnership, Hendry

forming a new alliance, Hendry, McCallum and Co., which continued owning and managing coastal steamers. Paton was clearly intending to put his energies and capital into the Coasting Motor Shipping Co. Ltd. which was incorporated on 16th January 1912 to exploit the potential of the oil engine. The company had a nominal capital of £50,000, of which Paton himself subscribed just over £8,000. There were no other notable shareholders, although two coal merchants named McAdam each subscribed £1,000.

Pioneers of the marine oil engine

Which was the first marine use of the oil engine is a vexed question, and Denmark, France, Germany, Netherlands, Russia, Sweden, Switzerland and the UK can all make good claims. Even A.C. Hardy, founder of the journal 'The Motor Ship' and evangelist for the cause of the marine oil engine, had difficulty sorting these claims in his detailed but obviously hastily-compiled 'History of Motor Shipping'. Intriguingly, the earliest record he cites is of a British example. The Thames sailing barge *Spinaway C* was completed at Ipswich in 1899 and immediately sailed round to the Isle of Wight where she was fitted with a Vosper hot-bulb engine. Sadly, this was only run once, as the barge was intended to trade up to Woodbridge on the River Deben, but her propellor became so entangled with weed in the river that her captain-owner insisted the engine was removed. Unlike this one, however, other experiments on the European continent were followed through. A small engine designed by Dr. Rudolf Diesel was fitted in a French canal barge some time before 1903. In 1904 Sulzer Brothers' first marine engine was installed in the cargo vessel *Venoge,* built to operate on Lake Geneva.

The *Eavestone,* built by Sir Raylton Dixon and Co. Ltd. in 1912 for Furness, Withy was the first British ocean-going motor ship, but was a rather unfortunate vessel. Her oil engine was built by Richardsons, Westgarth and Co. Ltd. under licence from a Belgian company, Carel Frères, who supplied various pieces from their works in Ghent. There were problems with liners and pistons, and *Eavestone* spent some time in the Azores disabled by an engine breakdown. The outbreak of war meant there was not the resources to carry on development work, and in 1915 the oil engine was replaced with a triple-expansion steam engine. *Eavestone* was lost on 3rd February 1917 when torpedoed 95 miles west of Fastnet by U 45. Exhaust gases from the engine were led up the derrick post which can be seen on the bridge deck: the funnel merely served two donkey boilers. *[Harry Hignett collection]*

From 1904, a considerable number of tankers - some surprisingly large - were built for use on Russian waterways and the Caspian Sea, and Russian and Swedish engineers made considerable advances in oil engine development.

There is not even a clear answer to the question of what was the first ocean-going motorship. At various points in his book, Hardy cites both the Italian cargo ship *Romagna* (678/1910) which had two Sulzer oil engines, and the Dutch Shell tanker *Vulcanus* (1,179/1910) completed at Amsterdam in December 1910.[2] An even better claimant must be the *Toiler* (1,659/1910), completed in September 1910 by Swan, Hunter for use on the Canadian lakes, and which had to cross the North Atlantic (see *Record* 12, page 249). The celebrated Danish motor ship *Selandia* (4,964/1912), completed in February 1912, was a relative latecomer, as was the first British example intended for deep-sea trading, Furness Withy's *Eavestone* (1,779/1912), completed in August 1912. It is noteworthy just how close were the completion dates of these oil-engined vessels.

Paton's fleet

Fitting an oil engine into a coastal ship was a particularly attractive proposition. There were potential savings in manpower, as firemen could be dispensed with, as well as savings on fuel. But perhaps most important was the additional carrying capacity for a given size and draft. This was made possible by the more compact engine room of the motor ship, which did not need boilers or space for coal bunkers, oil fuel being readily stored in odd spaces.

Surprisingly, no-one has published a history of the British motor coaster, at least not to the author's knowledge.[3] Claims as to the first example are hazy. Frank Bevis of Portsmouth had the Bolinders-engined *Ogarita* (95/1911) built at South Shields in 1911, probably for work in the Solent.[4] A Scottish candidate is the canal and estuarial trader *Peggy,* completed at Grangemouth in 1912.[5] However, Paton's enterprise put other British attempts to develop a motor coaster completely in the shade. His new company initially placed orders for 12 vessels, following up with a further six. The first, *Innisagra,* was launched on 25th April 1912.

The upper photograph shows the first of the Coasting Motor Shipping fleet, *Innisagra,* ready for launching from Peter MacGregor's yard at Kirkintilloch. Another vessel, probably the *Innisbeg* is behind her, with another to the left, possibly *Inniscroone.*

The lower photograph shows one of the vessels fitting out at Kirkintilloch, berthed alongside the slip seen above. This may well be the *Innisbeg,* which was launched on 31st May 1912, seven days after *Innisagra* had been completed. Another vessel - probably the *Innisdhu* - is in frame behind her.
[*East Dunbartonshire Council, P 1847 and P22231*]

Table 1: The types ordered by the Coasting Motor Shipping Co. Ltd.

Dimensions	Builder	Engine type	Names
65.6 x 18.4 x 8.6 feet	McGregor, Kirkintilloch	2-cyl. 2SCSA Bolinder	*Innisagra* *Inniscroone* *Innisdhu*
65.6 x 18.4 x 8.6 feet	McGregor, Kirkintilloch	4-cyl. 2SCSA Beardmore	*Innisbeg*
65.6 x 18.4 x 8.6 feet	McGregor, Kirkintilloch	2-cyl. 2SCSA Kromhout	*Inniseane* *Innisfree*
74.7 x 18.3 x 8.7 feet	McGregor, Kirkintilloch	2-cyl. 2SCSA Kromhout	*Innisglora* *Innishowen*
74.2 x 18.7 x 8.8 feet	Jeffrey, Alloa	2-cyl. Tuxham	*Innisinver* *Innisjura*
93.0 x 18.7 x 9.5 feet	Cran, Leith	2-cyl. 2SCSA Bolinder	*Inniskea*
99.0 x 18.8 x 8.4 feet	Cran, Leith	4-cyl. 2SCSA Beardmore	*Innislargie*
100.1 x 18.9 x 8.6 feet	Jeffrey, Alloa	4-cyl. 2SCSA Beardmore	*Innismurray* *Innisnee*
115.7 x 21.6 x 9.6 feet bridge forward	Chalmers, Rutherglen	4-cyl. 2SCSA Beardmore	*Innisshannon* *Innistrahull*
115.7 x 21.6 x 9.6 feet bridge aft	Chalmers, Rutherglen	4-cyl. 2SCSA Beardmore	*Innisulva* *Innisvera*

The types ordered are summarized in table 1. Broadly speaking, there were six length variations, and four types of engine fitted, and these variations meant that the largest homogenous group was just three strong. The four built by Chalmers were not uniform in design, although they had the same dimensions and engines. *Innisshannon* and *Innistrahull* initially had their bridge mounted right forward on the forecastle, whilst *Innisvera* and *Innisulva* had theirs on the poop. By the mid thirties, *Innisshannon* had lost her forward bridge in favour of an open structure conventionally placed aft. 'Shipbuilding and Shipping Record' published plans of an even larger type, with dimensions of 149.3 x 25.5 x 11.0 and Bolinders engines, and which looked like a conventional small coaster, but these were never built.

The vessels are sometimes described as 'motor puffers', but only the six smallest from Peter McGregor at Kirkintilloch truly merited this description. The dimensions of craft completed by this yard were limited to just 66 feet by the locks on the Forth and Clyde Canal. The two 74.7 feet vessels McGregor built were too large for these locks, so the bow section was dismantled and stowed in the hold, and the vessels were sent to Scott and Sons' yard at Bowling where McGregor's men completed assembly.

Trials of *Innisshannon* built by William Chalmers and Co. Ltd. at Rutherglen, on 13th June 1913. As later photographs of this long-lived coaster show, the bridge did not remain on the forecastle. At least 14 bodies are visible. *[Glasgow University Archives DC101/1226]*

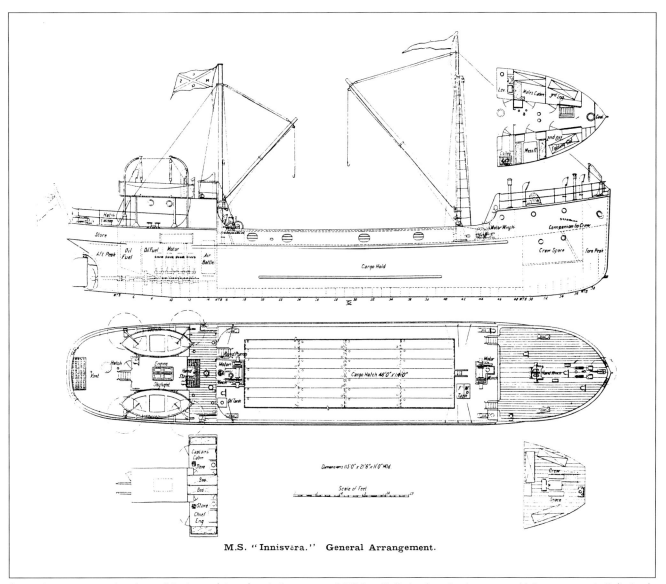

M.S. "Innisvera." General Arrangement.

General arrangement drawings of *Innisvera* (above) and of a proposed 149 feet Bolinders' engined coaster, which was never built (below).

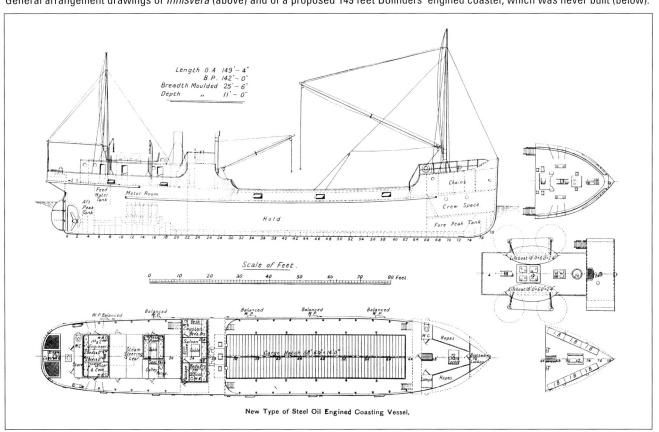

New Type of Steel Oil Engined Coasting Vessel.

In service: the problem of engineers

It is fortunate that a first-hand account of working as an engineer on these motor coasters has been published.[6] H.W. Bristow was working in a yacht-building yard in April 1912 when he was asked to go to Glasgow to be interviewed by John Paton and his eldest son, who told him to join the *Innisagra* which was fitting out at Kirkintilloch. *Innisagra* had a Swedish Bolinders hot-bulb engine, machinery which probably had the best reputation amongst contemporary oil engines, and an engineer had been sent from Stockholm to supervise its fitting. It is surprising, then, that several aspects of its installation were unsatisfactory. The tank for lubricating oil was not fixed firmly enough, and vibration caused airlocks in the oil pipes, leading to overheated bearings. Ordinary gas taps had been fitted to the fuel tanks, and these leaked. Lead pipes were used for connections to the bilge pump, and these tended to burst.

No satisfactory trials could be run in the Firth and Clyde Canal, so *Innisagra*'s first voyage to Belfast with a coal cargo was also her trial trip, an example of a lack of caution on Paton's part with what was essentially very new technology. At least the Bolinders engineer was on hand for this trip, and he had to solve the first problem. The cooling water tank had been filled near the end of the Canal, and as a result the water was brackish. As it dripped on to the cylinder, the water evaporated leaving a salt scale which resulted in heavy 'knocking'. The Swedish engineer had to stop the engine during the first night and chip the scale off the hot bulb. This was to be a recurring problem.

After the first voyage, Bristow was alone, but he does not record any untoward mechanical problems during his initial two months in *Innisagra*. Despite its small size, the ship made regular voyages across the North Channel, to Tory and Rathlin Islands, to the mainland of Ireland, to Scottish lighthouses with coal, and to distilleries on Islay and at Oban. In puffer fashion, *Innisagra* was often beached whilst horses and carts came alongside to discharge her coal cargo.

In June 1912 Bristow was asked to go to Leith as First Engineer on the Bolinders-engined *Inniskea,* completing at John Cran's yard. At 93 feet she was bigger than *Innisagra,* and had a crew of eight, including a Second Engineer. She voyaged even farther afield, with coal from the Forth to Wick and Kirkwall; beech logs from Loch Ness to Garston; and two 50-ton castings from Glasgow to Cammell, Laird's yard at Birkenhead. However, human problems dogged the voyages. The Second Engineer appointed was of little use. He was afraid of taking his watch below, was incapable of starting the engine, and managed to smash his thumb in the fuel pump. He was signed off at Garston, but his replacement was equally unsatisfactory. Next, John Paton's younger son took over, but he managed to repeat the problem of salt cooling water causing scaling on the cylinder head and hot bulb. Despite being the owner's son, he was made to chip off the scale.

Bristow was then asked to go back to *Innisagra.* It was unfortunate that both his ships were to come to grief. On 9th October, *Inniskea* was being towed back to Bowling for repairs to her engine which had broken down on a round trip to Tory Island, when the tow rope broke and she was wrecked on Islay. *Innisagra*'s turn came later that month. She had arrived in the Forth on a Sunday and was anchored beneath the railway bridge whilst Bristow was repairing an overheated big-end bearing, with the help of another marine engineer who he was training to drive the engine. The captain had the hatch covers off in readiness to discharge the cargo at Kirkcaldy the next morning. But the weather changed, and a gale sprang up which broke the anchor cable. The engine was started but - running on just one cylinder - it could not stop *Innisagra* from being driven up the Forth. As seas broke over her, the water got into her hold. An attempt to beach her on a patch of sand failed, and she ran into rocks below Kinghorn. *Innisagra* was eventually salved.

Mechanical problems claimed one more victim during Paton's ownership of the Innis boats, in September 1914 when the *Inniseane* foundered following an engine breakdown on a voyage from Ayr to the distillery at Bowmore, Islay. Bristow felt sorry for Paton over these losses, as he was a very considerate employer. Bristow points out that the *Innisagra* and *Inniskea* had made a number of fairly long passages between early May and November.

There were no more total losses in Paton's ownership, but there were other worrying incidents. On 12th December 1913, *Innistrahull* broke down west of Girvan, and was towed in but stranded on Girvan Bar, from where she was refloated a month later. *Innisglora* grounded in the Crinan Canal on 9th March 1914 whilst carrying grain for Oban. On 15th September 1914, *Innisfree* went ashore on Jura. *Innishowen* had to be towed into Stranraer by the steamer *Ashford* on 23rd September 1914. It is impossible at this distance to know if unreliability of engines or of engineers was responsible for these incidents. It is not surprising that, being watched carefully by other ship owners, they were perceived as unreliable.

Sales and eventual liquidation

As early as November 1914, the seven-month old *Innisvera* was sold to Danish owners who had some experience of motor vessels, the East Asiatic Company, for use in the West Indies. Four sales to the Russian Government followed in August 1915, and six to the Admiralty in March 1916 for use as water carriers. Two were sold to other commercial owners in 1917, three more in 1919. It seems that John Paton took what opportunities he could to dispose of his vessels. In selling on the rising market produced by the war, Paton was only doing what many more conventional shipowners were doing, taking a profit when he could from a business which was notoriously unpredictable. The sale to the Russian Government is believed to have realised £5,500 for each of the four vessels, which is probably only a little less than their original cost. These sales allowed the company's nominal capital to be reduced to £38,000 in March 1916. It is unlikely that the Admiralty paid any less. In December 1917 Paton would have got good prices for *Innisbeg* and *Inniscroone* from a Hull owner, and even better in April 1919 for the sale of *Innisagra* whilst he is known to have received £5,500 for *Innisdhu* and £6,250 for *Innishowen* in December 1919. There was a desperate shortage of coasters, many of which had been lost during the war without significant shipbuilding effort being devoted to their replacement. These four transactions, spread over five years, seem like considered sales after good offers had been received, rather than a 'fire sale' to fend off creditors. Once the last pair were sold the Coasting Motor Shipping Co. Ltd. was placed in voluntary liquidation late in December 1919. With income from the vessels that traded through the war plus sales revenue, Paton and his other investors probably

got most of their money back, although they are unlikely to have realised the rewards they expected. However, it is notable that neither Paton, who had been a shipowner for over 30 years, nor his sons returned to the business.

Careers and conversions

Despite their early troubles, the 'Innis' craft themselves seem to have been well built, as many had remarkably long lives. Three managed at least 36 years; *Inniscroone* was broken up after 50 years, and *Innisfree* after a remarkable 67 years. Ignoring the three sold to Russia whose fate is unkown, the average life of the 15 vessels was 27 years.[7] Three - *Innisagra*, *Inniseane* and *Inniskea* - were wrecked early, within 18 months of building. Together with a number of less serious incidents this was

indeed an unpropitious start (although the *Innisagra* was quickly salvaged) but, as further casualties were not clustered in the same way, it suggests human error arising from unfamiliarity with the machinery, and cannot necessarily be blamed on the vessels themselves. Given these early losses, the 27-year average life expectancy is impressive.

The five 'Innis' craft which survived Admiralty service readily found commercial buyers after the war, one Danish and the rest British. These had respectable careers, with the exception of the *Innisjura* which was wrecked in January 1921 in the Scottish waters to which she had returned. Indeed, *Innisshannon* and *Innisulva* became quite familiar around the coast in the 1920s and 1930s, and are the most frequently depicted in photographs.

Top: *Innisvera* on trials in the spring of 1914. Although to the same dimensions as *Innisshannon,* she had a wheelhouse placed conventionally aft. The occasion proved even more popular than the trials of *Innisshannon;* 17 bodies can be counted. *[Glasgow University Archives DC101/1224]*

Right: *Innisulva* leaving Terneuzen. A photograph of her at Torquay featured in *Record* 14, page 105. *[Chris F. Kleiss collection]*

The last two sold by Paton, *Innishowen* and *Innisdhu,* went to North Wales steel makers John Summers and Sons Ltd., although the *Innisdhu* was quickly sold on. *Innishowen* joined a fleet of small motor vessels which Summers had been building up since 1913. Their oil engines meant a shallow draft, which was useful when trading up the River Dee, loading galvanised steel at the company's wharf for the Mersey, where it would often be transferred to ocean-going ships.

There was considerable rebuilding of the craft during their lives, including *Innishowen* which was lengthened on the Dee in 1925. Judging by their owners' titles or known conversion work, four became tankers, employment probably suggested by the Admiralty's use of them as water carriers. As *Broiler,* the former *Innisbeg* carried linseed oil between Ipswich and the Thames and Medway.

At least four continents saw 'Innis' boats. Of those which stayed in Europe, two went to Denmark, including *Innisfree* which was to be the last survivor. The *Innisagra* went out to Africa. Late in life, *Innisshannon* went to Asia, working in the Red Sea out of Aden. The four sold to Russia may well have reached the same continent: *Innismurray* which became *Third International* is reported lost on what seems an extraordinary voyage, from Kem in the White Sea

Innisfree was the last known surviving Innis, not broken up until 1980. Here she is seen at Copenhagen in the early 1950s as the *Dangulf Lube*. Note the height of the mast. *[Søren Thørsoe collection]*

through Arctic waters to Kamchatka in the Bering Sea. Equally adventurous was *Innisvera*, which was specially prepared to cross the Atlantic to the Caribbean, and later served in South America.

Significantly in view of a reputation for unreliability gained during their early years, only three seem to have needed their engines replaced, although it may be that registration authorities were simply not informed about replacements. *Innishowen* and *Innisfree* had their Kromhouts taken out after 12 and 21 years, respectively, both receiving a third engine 19 and 27 years later. *Innisbeg* had the only Beardmore engine that needed replacing, after 14 years, whilst at least three Beardmores achieved almost 40 years of running.

War stories

One aspect of the trade to Northern Ireland was sinister: gun running. At 5.30 a.m. on 24th April 1914, *Innismurray* arrived at Donaghadee harbour to discharge 70 tons of rifles and ammunition destined for the Ulster Volunteer Force, which had been formed to resist any possibility of Irish home rule being imposed on Ulster. Volunteers from the Newtownards UVF brigades sealed off the harbour, detained customs officials, and dissuaded the few police who arrived from taking action. The arms were part of a total consignment of 25,000 rifles and three million rounds of ammunition which was landed that night at Larne, Bangor and Donaghadee. Did John Paton know what clandestine activities his *Innismurray* was engaged in? Perhaps like many Scots he had Unionist sympathies.

Little has been unearthed about the service of 'Innis' vessels sold to the Admiralty during the First World War. They were regarded as experimental, and probably the Admiralty were interested in the potential of the internal combustion engine. They were described as

water carriers, and presumably had tanks fitted in their holds to bring drinking and boiler water to steam-driven warships at various anchorages. Most frustrating is the lack of any details of the fate of *Innistrahull*, the only record being in the First World War Service List. RFA historian Tom Adams has pursued her fate diligently, but has not found anything in other official records. This may explain why 'Lloyds Register' continued to list her, along with the long wound-up Coasting Motor Shipping Co. Ltd., until 1935.

Innisdhu became a Second World War loss, probably due to a mine in the Thames Estuary. *Innisulva* was also a war victim, sunk at Le Havre, but was returned to service. Saddest case was the *Innishowen*, quite possibly the last victim of the Second World War, mined and sunk in Fano Bay, Denmark in May 1950, five years after the end of the European war.

Success or failure?

The Coasting Motor Shipping venture does not seem to have been the success that Paton hoped for. But this is different from dismissing it as a failure. The principle of applying oil engines to coasters was an excellent one, although it took until the 1930s before significant numbers began to appear in British ownership, and then at least another quarter century before the steam coaster expired. Paton was a brave pioneer, but perhaps over-bold in ordering 18 vessels with ten different engine and hull combinations. However, the crafts' subsequent often-long lives suggest that their hulls and - surprisingly in view of the reputation they gained - their machinery were fit for their intended service. This suggests strongly that the many early breakdowns, some of which proved fatal to the vessel, may have been due in considerable measure to the inexperience of those in the engine room.

Paton's biggest error was almost certainly not to ensure that enough adequately trained engineers were available. Bristow's accounts indicate a succession of steam engineers being appointed who were unable or unwilling to cope with oil engine technology. Paton had presumably overlooked the fact that, with the oil engine being almost unknown in British marine engineering practice, there was not, as there was with steam, a steady stream of engineers learning their trade in engine works or gaining experience under older men at sea. Poor installation, supervision and maintenance of the engines contributed to some of his early losses of craft, and certainly helped give the Innis craft a reputation for unreliability which, their subsequent history shows, was not totally deserved.

In the longer term, Paton's lack of success set back the cause of the oil engine as motive power for British coasters. Even at the time he was liquidating his company, Dutch owners of modest means - often captain-owners - were showing that their schooners took on a new lease of life when fitted with oil engines. The machinery was often from Germany, where the oil engine had been developed as a reliable way to propel submarines. So successful were these auxiliaries that the sails were soon dispensed with and the Dutch motor coaster emerged, to be remarkably successful and win a significant share of the British coastal trade. Dismissing the 'Innis' fleet as a failure allowed conservative British owners to ignore the potential of the oil engine, despite the Dutch example, and continue to rely on steam. Only in the 1930s did a few motor coaster pioneers, including Coast Lines, Everards of Greenhithe, William Robertson in Glasgow and William A. Wilson at Southampton start to fight the Dutch at their own game. But by then, the Dutch were almost unassailable, and the long-term decline of the British coaster was unstoppable.

John Paton and his Coasting Motor Shipping Co. Ltd. was a bold venture, flawed by not addressing the problem of manning the engine room of craft with novel machinery, especially important in view of the teething problems with marine oil engines. The principle of using oil engines in small coasters was wholly correct, and the hulls and engines of their craft were more than adequate, as prolonged, worldwide use has showed. Unfortunately, the widespread perception of the venture as being a failure significantly postponed the adoption of oil engines by UK owners, with serious consequences for British coastal shipping.

FLEET LIST

INNISAGRA

O.N. 133047 94g 56n 65.6 x 18.4 x 8.6 feet
Oil engine 2-cyl. 2SCSA by J. och C.G. Bolinders Mekaniska Verksted, Stockholm, Sweden; 80 BHP, 8 mph.
24.4.1912: Launched by Peter McGregor and Sons, Kirkintilloch (Yard No. 57).
24.5.1912: Registered in the ownership of the Coasting Motor Shipping Co. Ltd. (John M. Paton, manager), Glasgow as INNISAGRA
22.5.1912: Ran trials.
27.10.1912: Stranded near Kinghorn in the Firth of Forth whilst on a voyage from Northern Ireland to Kirkcaldy via the Forth and Clyde Canal with a cargo of whiting.
30.10.1912: Refloated, patched and towed to Leith for repairs.
24.4.1919: Sold to the African Association Ltd., Liverpool.
4.9.1919: Owners became the African and Eastern Trade Corporation Ltd., Liverpool.
26.9.1930: Register closed, vessel dismantled for use as a barge at Sierra Leone.

INNISBEG

O.N. 133064 95g 56n 65.6 x 18.4 x 8.7 feet
Oil engine 4-cyl. 2SCSA by William Beardmore and Co. Ltd., Coatbridge, Glasgow; 85 IHP, 8 knots.
1926: Kromhout oil engine 4-cyl. 2SCSA by D. Goedkoop junior, Amsterdam, Holland; 160 BHP, 8 knots.
31.5.1912: Launched by Peter McGregor and Sons, Kirkintilloch (Yard No. 59).
10.7.1912: Registered in the ownership of the Coasting Motor Shipping Co. Ltd. (John M. Paton, manager), Glasgow as INNISBEG.
7.12.1917: Sold to Harry L. Greig, Hull.
13.8.1918: Sold to the Innisbeg Shipping Co. Ltd. (Reginald M. Smith, manager), Hull.
22.11.1918: Foundered 500 yards off Westgate, Kent whilst on a voyage from St. Valery to Hull in ballast. Three of the crew of five were lost. Later salvaged.
6.8.1926: Registered in the ownership of the London and Rochester Trading Co. Ltd., Rochester as BROILER.
6.8.1948: Register closed on sale to France. However, there are reports that she was sold in 1947 and shipped as deck cargo from London to Valparaiso.

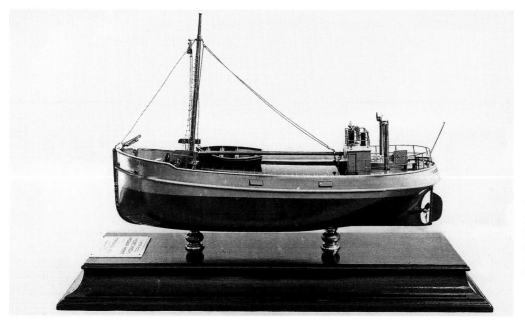

The first photograph of a model we can remember featuring in *Record,* and one which emphasises the smallness of the 66-foot motor puffers. It represents *Innisbeg.*

[*East Dunbartonshire Council, P2268]*

INNISCROONE
O.N. 133061 954g 56n
65.6 x 18.4 x 8.7 feet
Oil engine 2-cyl. 2SCSA by J. och C.G. Bolinders Mekaniska Verksted, Stockholm, Sweden; 80 BHP, 8 mph.
11.6.1912: Launched by Peter McGregor and Sons, Kirkintilloch (Yard No. 60).
1912: Completed for the Coasting Motor Shipping Co. Ltd. (John M. Paton, manager), Glasgow as INNISCROONE.
1917: Sold to Harry L. Greig, Hull.
1918: Sold to the London and Paris Marine Express Co. Ltd., Hull.
1921: Sold to Harry L. Greig, Hull.
8.8.1922: Acquired by Coast Lines Ltd., Liverpool and renamed TRURO TRADER.
11.3.1936: Sold to S.A. Portus, Liverpool.
1939: Sold to the Wadsworth Lightering and Coaling Co. Ltd., Liverpool.
10.1962: Sold to Arrowsmith for breaking up on the Mersey.

INNISDHU
O.N. 133086 95g 56n 65.7 x 18.4 x 8.7 feet
Oil engine 2-cyl. 2SCSA by J. och C.G. Bolinders Mekaniska Verksted, Stockholm, Sweden; 80 BHP, 8 mph.
25.9.1912: Launched by Peter McGregor and Sons, Kirkintilloch (Yard No. 58)
10.12.1912: Registered in the ownership of the Coasting Motor Shipping Co. Ltd. (John M. Paton, manager), Glasgow as INNISDHU.
16.12.1919: Sold to John Summers and Sons Ltd., Shotton, Flintshire for £5,500.
19.8.1922: Sold to Mackie and Co. Distillers Ltd., Glasgow.
31.1.1923: Sold to the National Benzole Co. Ltd., London.
6.4.1923: Renamed BEN OLLIVER.
25.4.1935: Renamed INNISDHU.
18.9.1935: Sold to Lloyds Albert Yard and Motor Packet Services Ltd. (Risdon A. Beazley, manager), Southampton.
28.4.1937: Sold to the New Medway Steam Packet Co. Ltd., Rochester.
20.9.1940: Sunk at Oldhaven on the Thames following an explosion, probably due to a mine, whilst on a voyage from Sheerness to Tilbury with general cargo. There were no survivors from her crew of four.
30.10.1940: Register closed. Sections of hull were later raised and placed ashore near Tilbury Fort.

INNISEANE
O.N. 133108 95g 56n 65.9 x 18.4 x 8.7 feet
Kromhout oil engine 2-cyl. 2SCSA by D. Goedkoop junior, Amsterdam, Holland; 110 IHP.
21.2.1913: Launched by Peter McGregor and Sons, Kirkintilloch (Yard No.61).
18.3.1913: Ran trials.
29.3.1913: Registered in the ownership of the Coasting Motor Shipping Co. Ltd. (John M. Paton, manager), Glasgow as INNISEANE.
21.9.1914: Foundered eight miles south east of Port Ellen, Islay after springing a leak and being driven broadside on following an engine breakdown whilst on a voyage from Ayr to Bowmore, Islay with a cargo of coal. Her five crew members took to her boat and were picked up by the trawler WRENTHORP (225/1906), which landed them at Campbeltown on 22.9.1914.
2.10.1914: Register closed.

INNISFREE
O.N. 133115 95g 56n 65.9 x 18.4 x 8.7 feet
1930: 129g 68n 84.6 x 18.3 x 8.6 feet
Kromhout oil engine 2-cyl. 2SCSA by D. Goedkoop junior, Amsterdam, Holland; 110 IHP.
1934: Oil engine 2-cyl. 2SCSA by A/S Burmeister & Wain, Copenhagen, Denmark.
1961: Oil engine 3-cyl. 4SCSA by Gamma, Frederikshavn, Denmark; 180 IHP.
3.4.1913: Launched by Peter McGregor and Sons, Kirkintilloch (Yard No. 62).
15.4.1913: Registered in the ownership of the Coasting Motor Shipping Co. Ltd. (John M. Paton, manager), Glasgow as INNISFREE.
7.9.1915: Sold to the Admiralty, London for use as a water carrier.[8]
24.11.1920: Sold to A/S Trafikant (P. Einarsen & M Andersen, managers), Bergen, Norway for £1,213 and renamed NUTTA.
1927: Sold to Master H. A. Christensen, Nykøbing Falster, Denmark, renamed FALSTER and portable tanks fitted in cargo hold.
20.1.1930: Sold to Eigil Qvist, København. Lengthened and converted into a tank vessel.
17.8.1933: Sold to Alfred Olsen Transport Co. A/S, København.
1947: Owners became Danish American Gulf Oil Transport Co. A/S, København.
21.2.1948: Renamed DANGULF LUBE.
1959: Sold to Hans Petersen, Aarøsund, Denmark and renamed INGER LUPE.
1961: New engine fitted.
8.2.1963: Sold to Wedellsborg Partrederi, Vedbæk, Denmark (Ebbe Wedell-Wedellsborg, Vedbaek and Ernst Gustav Baron Wedell-Wedellsborg, Thurø) and renamed HANNE WEDELL.
23.11.1965: During the conversion to a sand hopper/dredger the vessel sank in the port of Nykøbing Falster. Raised by the local rescue service.
1966: Conversion completed.
20.11.1967: Sold to Præstø Stenindustri A/S, Præstø, Denmark and renamed TANJA.
16.4.1973: Sold to T.J. Brunes, Holte, Denmark.
1980: Sold to Manfred Jensen for breaking up.
9.1980: Broken up at Esbjerg.

INNISGLORA

O.N. 133146 117g 77n 74.7 x 18.3 x 8.7 feet
Kromhout oil engine 2-cyl. 2SCDA by D. Goedkoop junior, Amsterdam, Holland; 110 IHP.
26.6.1913: Launched by Peter McGregor and Sons, Kirkintilloch (Yard No.63).
17.10.1913: Registered in the ownership of the Coasting Motor Shipping Co. Ltd. (John M. Paton, manager), Glasgow as INNISGLORA.
13.8.1915: Register closed on sale to the Russian Government.
1925: Deleted from *Lloyd's Register.*

INNISHOWEN

O.N. 133156 118g 79n 74.7 x 18.3 x 8.7 feet
1925: 146g 95n 88.7 x 18.6 x 8.6 feet
Kromhout oil engine 2-cyl. 2SCSA by D. Goedkoop junior, Amsterdam, Holland; 110 IHP.
1925: Oil engine 2-cyl. 2SCSA by J. och C.G. Bolinders Mekaniska Verksted, Stockholm, Sweden; 100 BHP.
1944: Kelvin oil engine 6-cyl. 4SCSA by Bergius Co. Ltd., Glasgow; 130 BHP.
28.8.1913: Launched by Peter McGregor and Sons, Kirkintilloch (Yard No.64).
4.11.1913: Registered in the ownership of the Coasting Motor Shipping Co. Ltd. (John M. Paton, manager), Glasgow as INNISHOWEN.
10.12.1919: Sold to John Summers and Sons Ltd., Shotton, Flintshire for £6,250.
19.5.1925: Re-registered following rebuilding by J. Crichton and Co., Connah's Quay.
19.4.1939: Sold to Risdon Beazley Ltd., Southampton.
10.12.1944: Re-registered following fitting of a new engine.
5.1947: Sold to Peter Chr. Petersen, Naestved, Denmark and renamed EVA PETERSEN.
4.5.1950: Mined and sunk in Fano Bay, Denmark whilst on a voyage from St. Olofsholm to Stege with a cargo of limestone. Her crew was rescued by the Swedish motor vessel WARUN (842/35).

The only photograph found of one of the four from Jeffrey of Alloa, the *Innisinver.*
[Glasgow University Archives DC101/1225]

INNISINVER

O.N. 133135 127g 65n 74.2 x 18.7 x 8.8 feet
Oil engine 2-cyl. by Tuxham Eng. Co., Valby, Copenhagen; 110 BHP, 8 knots.
20.5.1913: Launched by A. Jeffrey and Co., Alloa (Yard No. 7).
9.7.1913: Registered in the ownership of the Coasting Motor Shipping Co. Ltd. (John M. Paton, manager), Glasgow as INNISINVER.
14.8.1915: Sold to the Admiralty, London for use as a water carrier.[8]
27.4.1916: Register closed.
19.7.1920: Sold to Stick-Diesel Oil Engines Ltd., on behalf of Alexander Fergusson, for £3,800.
26.7.1920: Registered in the ownership of Alexander Fergusson, London.
11.11.1925: Sold to John Hornby and Sons (Shipbreakers) Ltd., Bradford.
26.3.1926: Sold to Henry S. Pulsford, Parkstone, Dorset.
11.9.1926: Owner became Honor Pulsford, Parkstone.
9.9.1930: Sank off Portland Bill after striking a submerged object whilst on a voyage from Par to Boulogne with a cargo of china clay. The four crew escaped in the ship's boat.
7.5.1931: Register closed.

INNISJURA

O.N. 133139 127g 65n 74.2 x 18.7 x 8.8 feet
Oil engine 2-cyl. by Tuxham Eng. Co., Valby, Copenhagen; 110 IHP, 8 knots.
19.6.1913: Launched by A. Jeffrey and Co., Alloa (Yard No. 8).
6.8.1913: Registered in the ownership of the Coasting Motor Shipping Co. Ltd. (John M. Paton, manager), Glasgow as INNISJURA.
2.10.1915: Sold to the Admiralty, London for use as a water carrier.[8]
13.3.1920: Sold to Renhold J. Frisk, Cardiff.
28.4.1920: Owner became the Mizel Shipping Co. Ltd. (Harold Davies and Renhold J. Frisk, managers), Cardiff.
10.1.1921: Wrecked in a gale at the entrance to Loch Broom whilst on a voyage from Loch Broom to Glasgow with a cargo of timber. The crew escaped in a boat and landed at Ullapool.
18.2.1921: Register closed.

INNISKEA

O.N. 133059 152g 90n 93.0 x 18.9 x 8.5 feet
Oil engine 2-cyl. 2SCSA by J. och C.G. Bolinders Mekaniska Verksted, Stockholm, Sweden; 120 BHP, 8 knots.
17.5.1912: Launched by John Cran and Co., Leith (Yard No. 88).
29.6.1912: Ran trials.
3.7.1912: Registered in the ownership of the Coasting Motor Shipping Co. Ltd. (John M. Paton, manager), Glasgow as INNISKEA.
9.10.1912: Wrecked on the Mull of Oa, Islay after breaking adrift from a tug whilst on passage from Tory Island to Glasgow in ballast. She had broken down and was being towed to Glasgow for repairs. The crew got ashore safely.
9.11.1912: Register closed.

INNISLARGIE

O.N. 133096 165g 94n 99.0 x 18.9 x 8.4 feet
Oil engine 4-cyl. 2SCSA by William Beardmore and Co. Ltd., Dalmuir, Glasgow; 30 NHP, 160 IHP, 7 knots.
1912: Launched by John Cran and Co., Leith (Yard No. 92).
17.1.1913: Ran trials.
20.1.1913: Registered in the ownership of the Coasting Motor Shipping Co. Ltd. (John M. Paton, manager), Glasgow as INNISLARGIE.
11.8.1915: Register closed on sale to the Russian Government.
1927: Deleted from *Lloyd's Register.*

INNISMURRAY

O.N. 133080 169g 95n 100.1 x 18.9 x 8.6 feet
Oil engine 4-cyl. 2SCSA by William Beardmore and Co. Ltd., Dalmuir, Glasgow; 120 BHP, 8 knots.
30.8.1912: Launched by A. Jeffrey and Co., Alloa (Yard No.4).
22.10.1912: Ran trials.
22.10.1912: Registered in the ownership of the Coasting Motor Shipping Co. Ltd. (John M. Paton, manager), Glasgow as INNISMURRAY.
13.8.1915: Register closed on sale to the Russian Government.

After the Bolshevik revolution renamed THIRD INTERNATIONAL
9.1929: Foundered off Solovetsky whilst on a voyage from Kem to Kamchatka.

INNISNEE

O.N. 133088 170g 95n 100.3 x 18.9 x 8.6 feet
Oil engine 4-cyl. 2SCSA by William Beardmore and Co. Ltd., Dalmuir, Glasgow; 120 BHP, 8 knots.
11.9.1912: Launched by A. Jeffrey and Co., Alloa (Yard No.5).
27.12.1912: Registered in the ownership of the Coasting Motor Shipping Co. Ltd. (John M. Paton, manager), Glasgow as INNISNEE.
19.8.1915: Register closed on sale to the Russian Government.
1927: Deleted from *Lloyd's Register.*

INNISSHANNON

O.N. 133128 238g 143n 115.7 x 21.6 x 9.6 feet
Oil engine 4-cyl. 2SCSA by William Beardmore and Co. Ltd., Dalmuir, Glasgow; 26 NHP, 220 IHP, 8 knots.
2.4.1913: Launched by William Chalmers and Co. Ltd., Rutherglen, Glasgow (Yard No. 164).
13.6.1913: Ran trials.
23.6.1913: Registered in the ownership of the Coasting Motor Shipping Co. Ltd. (John M. Paton, manager), Glasgow as INNISSHANNON.
16.9.1915: Sold to the Admiralty, London for use as a water carrier and given the pennant number X. 32.[8]
14.10.1920: Handed over to the Disposal Board.
23.2.1921: Sold to Max S. Hilton, London for £5,250.
6.5.1924: Sold to C. Shaw Lovell and Sons Ltd. (Algernon H. Philpot, manager), London.
9.7.1947: Sold to United Coasters Ltd. (George A. Tom and Co. Ltd., managers), London.
12.1.1948: Renamed STRATTON CROFT.
20.1.1950: Sold to Sheikh Ali Mohamed Omer Bazara trading as the Arab Navigation and Transport Co., Aden.
15.5.1950: Renamed ARAB NAVIGATOR.
3.8.1952: Wrecked amongst the Farasan Islands, south of Jeddah in the Red Sea after an engine breakdown.
27.11.1952: Register closed.

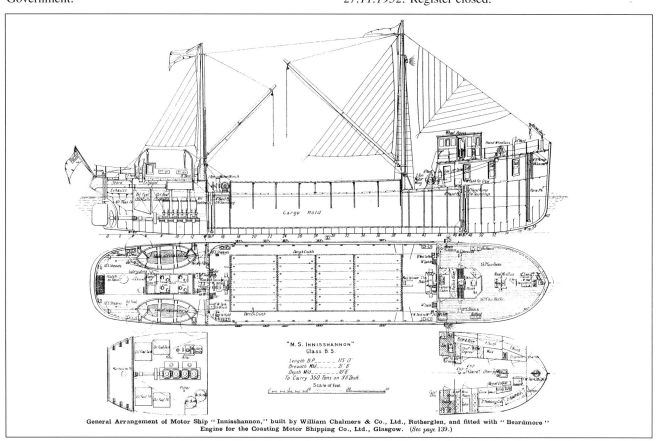

General arrangement drawing of the *Innisshannon*.

INNISTRAHULL

O.N. 133144 238g 143n 115.8 x 21.6 x 9.6 feet
Oil engine 4-cyl. 2SCSA by William Beardmore and Co. Ltd., Dalmuir, Glasgow; 26 NHP, 220 IHP, 8 knots.
9.5.1913: Launched by William Chalmers and Co. Ltd., Rutherglen, Glasow (Yard No. 165).
25.6.1913: Ran trials.
21.8.1913: Registered in the ownership of the Coasting Motor Shipping Co. Ltd. (John M. Paton, manager), Glasgow as INNISTRAHULL.
14.3.1916: Sold to the Admiralty, London for use as a water carrier.
27.4.1916: Register closed.
1916: Lost on Admiralty service.
INNISTRAHULL was erroneously listed in *Lloyd's Register* until 1935, as owned by Coasting Motor Shipping Co. Ltd.

INNISULVA

O.N. 136338 235g 143n 115.8 x 21.6 x 9.5 feet
Oil engine 4-cyl. 2SCSA by William Beardmore and Co. Ltd., Dalmuir, Glasgow; 220 IHP, 8 knots.
16.4.1914: Launched by William Chalmers and Co. Ltd., Rutherglen, Glasgow (Yard No. 168).
3.12.1914: Registered in the ownership of the Coasting Motor Shipping Co. Ltd. (John M. Paton, manager), Glasgow as INNISULVA.
20.9.1915: Sold to the Admiralty, London for use as a water carrier.[8]
21.4.1920: Sold to Renhold J. Frisk, Cardiff.
28.4.1920: Owners became the Mizel Shipping Co. Ltd. (Harold Davies and Renhold J. Frisk, managers), Cardiff.
19.7.1924: Sold to C. Shaw Lovell and Sons Ltd. (Algernon H. Philpot, manager), London.
12.6.1940: Abandoned at Paris and seized by German forces. One member of the crew of five became a prisoner of war.
30.6.1942: Condemned by the Hamburg Prize Court.
14.7.1942: Register closed.
30.1.1946: Found sunk at Quai Garonne Vieux, Le Havre.
13.12.1946: Refloated by the French Navy.
1948: Sold to Société Havraise Industrielle et Navale, Le Havre and under repair in 1949, but no further details found.

Innistrahull on trials. So great seems to have been the interest in these motor coasters that on this occasion at least 25 people have come for the ride. *[Glasgow University Archives DC101/1227]*

INNISVERA

O.N. 136291 238g 143n 115.7 x 21.6 x 9.6 feet
Oil engine 4-cyl. 2SCSA by William Beardmore and Co. Ltd., Coatbridge, Glasgow; 220 IHP, 8 knots.
3.3.1914: Launched by William Chalmers and Co. Ltd., Rutherglen, Glasgow (Yard No. 167).
28.5.1914: Registered in the ownership of the Coasting Motor Shipping Co. Ltd. (John M. Paton, manager), Glasgow as INNISVERA.
10.1914: Sold to A/S Det Østasiatiske Kompagni (the Danish East Asiatic Company), Copenhagen, Denmark and renamed ANHOLT.
14.1.1915: After alterations, left Milford Haven for St. Thomas West Indies Islands, the Caribbean (now the Virgin Islands). Used for domestic trading between the islands St. Thomas, St. Jan and St. Croix.
1916: Heavily damaged by grounding in the port of St. Thomas during a hurricane. Declared a total loss and abandoned.
18.10.1917: Wreck was disposed of to local interests in Puerto Rico.
1917: Sold to Pierce Navigation Co. Inc., New York, USA and renamed SOLARINA.
1920: Owners became the Pierce Oil Corporation, New York.
1926: Owners became the Pierce Petroleum Corporation, New York.
1926: Sold to Alberto Vales & Co., Rio de Janeiro.
24.10.1926: Sank after her cargo of gasoline caught fire in Rio de Janeiro. Salvaged and repaired.
1927: Sold to J.E. Cabieses, Vera Cruz, Mexico and renamed MARINERO.
1930: Sold to S.C. Loveland Co. Inc., Philadelphia, USA and renamed SOLARINA.
1943: Sold to the Honduras Shipping Co., Tegucigalpa.
10.12.1952: Foundered in bad weather 25 miles south west of Buenaventura, Colombia.

Comparing this view of the *Innisshannon* at Torquay with that of her sister opposite shows the extent to which she was rebuilt. Where and when is not known. *[David Eeles]*

Notes

1. Early editions of Charles Waines' seminal work 'Steam Coasters and Short Sea Traders' maintain that '...the project failed and the vessels were sold', although later editions are more cautious. A.I. Bowman in his 'Kirkintilloch Shipbuilding' says that 'The 'Innis' boats were not a success.'
2. Hardy gives building dates for the *Romagna* of both 1909 (page 18) and 1911 (page 341), claiming she was lost on her maiden voyage when her cargo shifted. 'Lloyd's Register' for 1911 gives a building date of 1910, unfortunately with no month. She foundered on 24th November 1911 during a voyage from Ravenna to Trieste with general cargo..
3. Like too many authors, Hardy largely ignores coastal ships, and the only mention of the 'Innis' boats in 'History of Motorshipping' is of two remaining in service into the 1930s.
4. See the author's 'Cambrian Coasters'.
5. In 'Kirkintilloch Shipbuilding' Bowman maintains that *Peggy,* has as good a claim as Paton's boats to be the first 'motor puffer', but offers no date for her completion. Paton's first, *Innisagra,* ran trials in May 1912.

6. Bristow HW. 'Pioneer Motor Coasters', *Sea Breezes,* 1950, X, 346-350
7. The 27 years is undoubtedly an under-estimate. *Innisbeg* and *Innisulva* are known to have survived until at least 1948, their fates being unknown although the former was probably scrapped in the late 1940s; whilst *Innisagra's* hull survived in use as a barge after 1930. Neither can inadequacies of their hull be blamed for the losses of *Innisdhu* and *Inishowen.*
8. This is the date of entering service according to Admiralty records. However, the ships' closed registers - also official documents and ones which aim to record sales to the day, and often the exact hour - gives 11.3.1916 for *Innisjura,* and 14.3.1916 for *Innisfree, Innisinver, Innisshannon* and *Innisulva.*

SOURCES AND ACKNOWLEDGEMENTS

Photographs are from the collection of John Clarkson unless otherwise credited. We thank all who gave permission for their photographs to be used, and for help in finding photographs. We are particularly grateful to Tony Smith, Jim McFaul and David Whiteside of the World Ship Photo Library; to Ian Farquhar, Bill Laxon, Peter Newall, Ivor Rooke, William Schell, George Scott; to David Hodge and Bob Todd of the National Maritime Museum; Dr David Jenkins of the National Museums and Galleries of Wales; and other museums and institutions listed.

Research sources have included the *Registers* of William Schell and Tony Starke, *Lloyd's Register, Lloyd's Confidential Index, Lloyd's War Losses, Mercantile Navy Lists,* and *Marine News.* Paricular thanks also to William Schell and John Bartlett for various information.

Canadian Pacific's Beavers
George Musk, *Canadian Pacific Afloat* 1883-1968, Canadian Pacific, 1968; George Musk, *Canadian Pacific: the Story of the Famous Shipping Line,* David and Charles, Newton Abbot, 1981.

The Liberty Liners
Paolo Piccione and Bohdan Huras have been particularly helpful while the author has been researching this article. Others to whom thanks are due are Maurizio Eliseo; Alberto Bisagno; and Declan Barriskill of the Guildhall Library, London. In addition, the following have been consulted: *Lloyd's Voyage Records; Lloyd's Registers; Lloyd's List;* J. W. Bull, *An Introduction To Safety At Sea,* Brown, Son and Ferguson, Ltd., Glasgow, 1966; Juan Carlos Díaz Lorenzo, *Los Trasatlánticos de la Emigración* Gobierno de Canarias, 1993; Maurizio Eliseo and Paolo Piccione, *The Costa Liners,* Carmania Press, 1997; Maurizio Eliseo and Paolo Piccione, *Transatlantici,* Tormena Editore, 2001; I.G. Stewart *Liberty Ships In Peacetime,* Ian Stewart Marine Publications, 1992; W.H. Mitchell and L.A. Sawyer *Liberty Ships,* Lloyd's of London Press, 1970.

The Innis boats
Thanks to Tom Adams, David Burrell, Raymond Counter (who wrote about these vessels in the journal *Tees Packet*), David Eeles, David Hocquard, David Jenkins, Chris Kleiss, Bill Lind, Tony Smith, Soren Thorsoe, and Ian Wilson. Consulted were various editions of *Shipbuilding and Shipping Record,* and A.I. Bowman, *Kirkintilloch Shipbuilding,* Strathkelvin District Libraries, Glasgow.

Renfrew retrospective
Thanks to Rear Admiral Roger Morris and Dr. Richard Osborne of the World Ship Society. Much consulted was: F.J. Dittmar and J.J. Colledge, *British Warships 1914-1919,* Ian Allan, Shepperton, 1972.

Remember the *Wendy Ann?*
Former Harry Rose tug masters Ron Wills and John Hayes; Michael Bolson, Bob Kent, Chris Wood and Jack Bailey are thanked for their reminiscences; and David Watkins (Poole Museum Services), Clive Guthrie and John Clarkson for help with photographs and information.

More days, more dollars
Books consulted include Course A.G. *The Wheel's Kick and the Wind's Song;* Mowat H.G. *Lonely Ships;* Hurst A. A. *Square-Riggers: the Final Epoch*; and various editions of *Sea Breezes.*

RENFREW RETROSPECTIVE
Colin Campbell and Roy Fenton

These recently-unearthed photographs allow us to look back at a tiny part of the output of a neglected Scottish shipbuilder, Lobnitz and Co. Ltd. of West Yard, Renfrew. Dating from around 1838, the yard came under the control of a James Henderson in 1847. In 1857, Henderson took on Henry Lobnitz, who had been born at Fredericia in Jutland, and who gradually came to control the company. The company was known as Henderson, Coulborn and Co., from 1861 and then - reflecting Henry Lobnitz's influence - Lobnitz, Coulborn and Co. In 1895 the title became Lobnitz and Co. Ltd., but Henry Lobnitz died in 1896.

The yard's output was immense: no fewer than 1,200 vessels had been built by 1957 when an amalgamation with a neighbouring shipbuilder produced Simons-Lobnitz Ltd. From early on the West Yard had specialised in dredgers, building over one hundred craft for the Suez Canal Company alone.

Three years after the merger with rival dredger builders William Simons and Co., the combined company became part of the Weir Group, but was almost immediately shut down. In his masterly 'Song of the Clyde' shipbuilding historian Fred Walker leaves no doubt about how he felt about the closure: '...it was in national terms a tragedy almost unequalled on the Clyde. A unique service which was unequalled in scope and possessed hard-earned expertise in the design, building and selling of

dredgers was lost to Britain.'

The ships illustrated here mainly reflect Lobnitz's output of 39 ships for the Admiralty during the First World War. Mercantile-minded *Record* readers will have to forgive the slight naval tinge to some of these: all have a mercantile pedigree.

The remarkable craft pictured opposite top was the *Derocheuse*, launched in October 1887 for the Suez Canal Company, as Lobnitz yard number 300. It was claimed to be the first application of rock cutting principles to a bucket dredger. Presumably, it was to serve in both roles, there being more steady work for a dredger than a rock cutter. The ten rock cutters were mounted forward, in a lattice structure that gave some cause for concern over stability during her delivery voyage. She accomplished it successfully, however, and it was claimed by Lobnitz 50 years later that *Derocheuse* was still working as a bucket dredger. It would interesting to know how her rock cutters worked, and how long she survived.

Hakuai Maru (2,629/1898, yard number 471) is another intriguing vessel (opposite bottom). Her initial owner is given as the Red Cross Society of Japan, and the cross on her funnel suggests she was completed as a hospital ship, presumably for service during the Russo-Japanese War. By 1900 she was in commercial service with Nippon Yusen Kaisha, suggesting that she was ordered by this line, and converted to a hospital ship before

completion. Sold by NYK in 1926, she had a variety of other Japanese owners, and shared the fate of so many Japanese ships of her period. On 18th June 1945 she was torpedoed off the Kurile Islands by US Submarine *Apogon*.

The photograph was presumably taken in Lobnitz's fitting out basin. In the foreground is the tug *Leso,* built by the yard in 1893

Although her 12-pounder gun is clearly visible, the *James Caton* (below) was built to a mercantile design, that of the trawler *Lord Mersey*, completed in 1916 by Cochrane and Sons Ltd. of Selby. Lobnitz built five other 'Mersey' class trawlers for the Admiralty: *Richard Colliver* (1917), *Thomas Corwall, Isaac Chant, Henry Cramwell* and *Thomas Cruize* (all 1918). *James Caton,* launched in August 1918 as yard number 822, could have seen very little war service. The trawler was sold for fishing purposes, becoming the French *Emilie Pierre* in 1921 and later the *St. Pierre D'Alcantara*. In 1940 she was requisitioned by the French Navy for auxiliary patrol service, but was paid off in October. *St. Pierre D'Alcantara* was sunk off Ouessant on 9th July 1941, but refloated. She was taken over by the Germans in 1942, and commissioned into the Kriegsmarine in August 1943 as the Vorpostenboot *V.201*. Found damaged in 1945, she was broken up. She had served in three different navies during her career. For more on the 'Merseys', see *Record* 2, pages 76 to 81.

The choice of Lobnitz to build naval oilers is an interesting one, as it is not clear whether they had any prior experience of constructing tank vessels. Presumably it was thought that a yard that could build hoppers was quite capable of building a vessel with oil tanks. Certainly, the Admiralty took over a number of hoppers built by the other specialist Clyde yards, Simons and Fleming and

Ferguson, and converted them to oilers. It even took over a dredger on the stocks at Renfrew and had it completed as an oiler, giving it one of the ugliest names imaginable, *Dredgol*.

The 17 oilers built for the Admiralty were mostly given names with the suffix 'ol' preceded by a tree name, in this case *Larchol* (yard number 818): Lobnitz's other example

being *Limol*. Launched late in 1917, these vessels gave long service, or at least survived into a ripe old age. Both were delivered to shipbreakers on 23rd August 1959, *Larchol* to Belgian scrappers and *Limol* to Briton Ferry. Several of these distinctive vessels passed into mercantile service after the Second World War. *Larchol* was photographed passing Rothesay Dock.

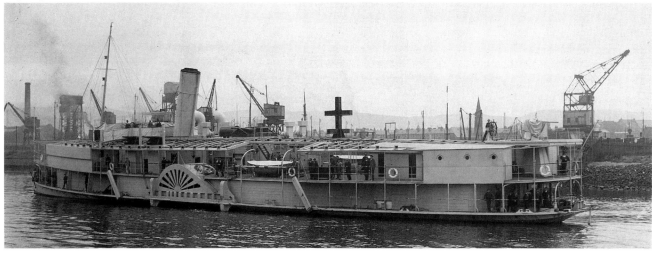

Built in 1917, *HP8* (above) and *HP9* (below) were paddle hospital ships, part of an order shared between six Scottish and north east English yards. As many as 17 were built, the first two from Dennys (*HP1* and *HP2*) being hulls completing for the Irrawaddy Flotilla Company which were taken over by the War Office in

1915. They were shallow-drafted vessels for the campaign in Mesopotamia, hurriedly converted or ordered following a scandal about lack of provision for treating wounded. According to some sources they were shipped out dismantled and assembled at Abadan, but the way the forward structure has been cased in suggests

HP8 and *HP9* were going out under their own steam. It is hoped they arrived in time to help some of the many casualties of the messy campaign in the Middle East (history currently repeating itself in this region). Lobnitz yard numbers were 816 and 817.

P60 (yard number 811) was one of two river craft also built for the Mesopotamian campaign, and designed to serve on the rivers Tigris and Euphrates (above). Lobnitz built another (P61), whilst Beardmore built two (P50 and P51), with Caird completing six more (P52 to P57). Armament is given as one three-pounder, the mounting for this being in place on the foredeck. Again, they were to be shipped and assembled at Abadan or Basra. P60, its sister P61, HP8 and HP9 were transferred to the Royal Indian Marine in 1919, but thereafter quickly disappear from the records.

There is much interesting shipbuilding clutter in the background, not least the sheerlegs.

If any excuse is needed for including the extraordinary HMS Slinger, it is that she was building as a steam hopper, and was taken over for conversion to an 'experimental catapult ship' as Dittmar and Colledge describe her (below). Their voluminous and invaluable 'British Warships 1914-1919' is silent on the outcome of her experiments, but does record that she was sold to M.S. Hilton in October 1919.

REMEMBER THE WENDY ANN?
Stephen Carter

From 1947 to 1996 visitors to the busy Port of Poole in Dorset admired the *Wendy Ann,* the local tug. Always immaculately maintained and usually moored just below the Town Bridge when not working; they were for nearly 50 years an integral part of the Poole waterfront scene. I say 'they' because there was not one but five tugs named *Wendy Ann* during this period and the owner's practice of naming every one after his daughter has over the years caused much confusion amongst shipping enthusiasts.

Harry Rose, who lived at 36 Queens Avenue, Bournemouth and later at Parkstone, was by all accounts quite a character. He was brought up in India, where his father managed a large jute factory, and he became a test rider and driver with the Talbot motor company, which no doubt suited his taste for fast motoring. He raced at Brooklands, and later owned and competed in a collection of vintage sports cars including a Le Mans Bentley and a supercharged Bentley. During the Second World War Harry, because of his engineering background, was - according to one of his great friends Major Jack Bailey - engaged on civilian work for the war effort. In 1947 Harry Rose bought an ex-Admiralty steam pinnace and converted this 54-foot long wooden vessel into a tug, registered her at Poole and named her *Wendy Ann* after his daughter. With this little tug he began a business which was to serve him well for many years. After the war, Poole harbour was booming and there was much shipping traffic, but in the early days Harry used to tow anything he could, and one of the jobs undertaken was towing a Morecambe Bay prawner (a type of sailing fishing boat used in the north west of England, many of which were converted to yachts because of their fine sailing qualities) from Christchurch to Poole for the vessel's new owners. Poole Harbour Commissioners owned a steam tug, the 80-ton, 74-foot *Peter Joliffe,* but much of this vessel's time was taken up attending to the dredger and hopper barge. With the building of a new coal-fired power station above the Town Bridge at Poole, collier traffic increased dramatically and all the colliers required the services of a tug to assist them through the bridge.

Harry Rose was looking to the future and he had the steam engine removed and replaced by a brand new Gleniffer diesel of about 120 BHP. This not only meant that the vessel could be started at short notice but it also allowed engine control from the wheelhouse, a great advantage.

When he started his business or very shortly afterwards, Harry was able to employ as a tug master a man with a great knowledge of Poole Harbour, Ivor Holloway. Ivor had been coxswain of the Poole pilot boat and during the busy war years had also acted as pilot. He left the pilotage service and remained with Harry Rose until the tugs were sold to the Harbour Commissioners in 1981, long after Harry's death. Ivor had the advantage of not only being very conversant with Poole Harbour itself but, equally importantly, knew the right people, the shipmasters and agents. In the early years Harry's wife Muriel also often helped on the tugs in busy periods, but Ivor was something of a traditionalist and would not countenance a woman aboard the tug - bad luck, so it was a case of either she went or he did.

Harry Rose with an unknown lady in the wheelhouse of one of his tugs. *[Author's collection]*

Something new, something old

With business booming a new tug was ordered from the local shipyard of J. Bolson and Sons Ltd. Launched in 1950 this steel vessel was fitted with a 200 BHP Blackstone engine which gave a speed of nine knots and a bollard pull of three tons. Although this seems very low by modern tug standards, it would be more than adequate for assisting the type and size of ships using Poole at the time.

The next tug was far from new, and in fact was not even built as a tug. In 1951 Harry bought the ex-Liverpool Port Health Authority launch *Moyles,* a steel twin-screw vessel built in 1927 at Northwich. The *Moyles* was originally fitted with two Gardner 90 BHP semi-diesels with engine room control. Harry Rose had the vessel completely gutted and refitted. Power came from two Gleniffer DH6 engines driving twin 42-inch

diameter four-bladed propellers, and this gave a bollard pull of four tons. Harry designed and fitted his own form of bridge control for the engines. This vessel eventually entered service in 1952 as the *Wendy Ann II.* Although carrying the new name, the tug was not officially registered as such until June 1956 when the registration was transferred to Poole. It is thought that the original wooden pinnace was disposed of when this vessel entered service. The *Wendy Ann II* attended the Coronation Review at Portsmouth in 1953. The ex-*Moyles* did not remain in the fleet for very long, however, and was sold to the British Dredging Corporation in 1957. During the rebuild this vessel was fitted with keel cooling and it was found that the engines were prone to overheating during a static pull with no water flowing over the keel cooling pipes.

Top: the second *Wendy Ann,* built at Poole in 1950.
[Author's collection]

Right: *Moyles* newly-built at W.J. Yarwood's shipyard, Northwich.
[Clive Guthrie collection]

Above: motor tug *C129* at W.J. Yarwood's shipyard in 1940. *[Clive Guthrie collection]*

Below: the 1950-built *Wendy Ann* and *Wendy Ann 2* (ex *C129*) at Poole Quay. *[Poole Museums]*

Secondhand acquisitions

In 1955 the Admiralty tug *C129* was acquired and initially named *Wendy Ann III*. This was another product of Northwich, built in 1940. She was a single-screw vessel fitted with a Petter SS-type diesel engine. During the war years the *C129* had been based at Devonport and was transferred to Portland in 1946. With the size of ships using Poole increasing, in 1963 Harry Rose had the original engine removed and a new Lister Blackstone engine fitted. The engine had a Blackstone gearbox with a 3 to 1 reduction and in order to gain the required thrust the tug was fitted with an unusual five-bladed propeller to fit in the restricted propeller aperture. The initial conversion was not entirely successful. The hull was considered to be quite lightly built and the new machinery set up excessive vibrations throughout the vessel. To cure this problem the engine was refitted on six Metalastic Cushymount mountings and the gearbox was connected to the engine by a cardan shaft with flexible couplings at each end. All other engine connections were altered to flexible pipework and these modifications completely cured the problems. A side effect of the conversion was a considerable reduction in engine noise. On completion of the conversion the vessel was renamed *Wendy Ann 2* although it is very probable that she had become the *Wendy Ann II* after the sale of the ex *Moyles* in 1957. The registration documents record the name with the number 2 but it was sometimes painted as the Roman II, adding to the general confusion. In any case the bollard pull was now a useful five tons, which was probably about double the original figure.

In late June 1970 Harry Rose acquired his last and biggest tug. From London Tugs Ltd. he bought the *Vespa*. This was one of a type used for both lighterage and ship towage on the Thames and had been built by Alexander Hall of Aberdeen in 1934 as the *Brodstone* for

Wendy Ann 2 in Poole Harbour Commissioners' ownership at Poole, 11th April 1984. *[J. and M. Clarkson]*

Frederick Leyland Ltd. of Liverpool, although the vessel was employed in London. In 1935 she was transferred to a subsidiary company, Blackfriars Lighterage, and renamed *Evelene Brodstone*. In 1946 she was bought by the well-known London tug owners Gaselee and Son Ltd. who renamed her *Vespa*. The tug was originally fitted with a Mirrlees, Bickerton and Day engine. In 1953 during Gaselee ownership the tug was run down and sunk in Gallions Reach by the Swedish cargo vessel *Malmo*. After salvage Gaselee fitted a 525 BHP British Polar engine and returned the tug to service. In 1965 Gaselee sold their ship towing interests and their four largest tugs, including the *Vespa*, to Ship Towage (London) Ltd. which in turn became London Tugs Ltd. in 1969. Harry Rose purchased this vessel in June 1970 and the *Vespa* was towed from London to Poole by the *Sun XXVI* on the 6th July 1970. The tug was not immediately renamed. Harry Rose had plans once again to completely refit the vessel, but tragically he was not to see it happen. On Sunday 20th September Harry had been out for a test drive in his newly restored turbo-charged Mark VI Special Bentley and then proceeded to Poole to check on his tugs. He collapsed and died on Poole Quay alongside his three tugboats, at the age of 61.

This was far from the end of the towage business, however. Initially his wife Muriel took over the company and later his daughter Wendy Ann Shoesmith took the reins of the business, ably assisted by Ivor Holloway who became a director after Harry's death. In 1972 the *Vespa* went to Husbands Shipyard at Marchwood for the major rebuild that Harry had planned. Out came the engine-room-controlled British Polar to be replaced by a bridge-controlled 600 BHP Blackstone with a 3 to 1 Blackstone gearbox driving a 6 foot 6 inch diameter propeller. Out came the chain and rod steering gear to be replaced by Donkin-powered hydraulic gear. A new wheelhouse was fitted and the accommodation was completely rebuilt. These modifications gave a bollard pull in excess of eight tons and made for a very handy vessel. Strangely she was not immediately renamed *Wendy Ann* and it would appear that this did not happen until the sale of the Bolsons-built *Wendy Ann* of 1950, which occurred in 1974 when this vessel was sold to London owners to become the *Andrew II*. The *Vespa* then became the *Wendy Ann* whilst the ex *C129* remained *Wendy Ann 2*.

Towage, salvage and maintenance

Up until the 1960s there was a steady stream of shipping in Poole. Stephenson Clark colliers brought coal for Poole Gas Works and after the construction of the Poole Power Station colliers were towed through Poole Bridge. Later, when the power station was converted to burn oil fuel, the colliers were replaced by coastal tankers. The first generation of ro-ro ships using Poole also brought work for Harry Rose's tugs, as did the various movements and launches at Bolsons Shipyard. After the sale of the Commissioners tug, Harry Rose was also employed to tow the Commissioners hopper barge to sea for dumping. In 1973 the *Wendy Ann 2* (ex *C129*) ran aground on Parkstone Shoal whilst trying to refloat the ro-ro *Poole Antelope* which had grounded on the shoal. The tug managed to refloat herself and suffered only slight chipping of her propeller blades. The ferry was eventually freed by the tug with the assistance of the *Vespa*. Like any tug owner Harry Rose was quick off the mark for a salvage job. In fact, the other main tug master of long-standing, Ron Wills, had been second mate on the famous salvage tug *Turmoil* of *Flying Enterprise* fame before taking a master's job with Harry Rose after his marriage. Ron Wills said that it was something of a shock to move from a tug with a crew of over 30 to one with a crew of three. Another tug master of long-standing, John Hayes had also been in the Poole pilot boats and acted as pilot on occasions, and he also joined the tugs, following Ivor Holloway.

Shipping casualties were often quite numerous even if of a minor nature. Cosens paddle steamers were more than once rescued by Harry's tugs, which led to salvage claims. In 1966 Cosen's last paddler, the *Embassy*, suffered a major problem to a paddle wheel and had to eventually anchor off Milford-on-Sea. Harry Rose's tugs were called and the *Wendy Ann* arrived at 8.45pm and took the vessel in tow for Poole, which was eventually reached at 2 am the following morning. Interestingly, one report of this incident suggests that it was the *Wendy Ann* (which at this stage of the company's history would be the 200 BHP, 1951 Bolson built vessel), with the *Wendy Ann 2* assisting when Poole was reached. However, another account suggests the tugs were the other way round, showing the confusion which occurred over the years with the naming and renaming policy of the tugs. Cosens were regular users of the service in Poole, assistance often being needed to lift the paddlers off the quay if the wind was pinning them on.

Harry Rose was an astute operator, however, and his bread and butter work of firstly colliers and then Shell tankers going through the bridge to Poole Power Station was secured partly by having no salvage claim clauses in contracts with the ship owners. Another task undertaken by the company was the maintenance of the sewage outfall buoys for the various local authorities and all the buoys between Poole Head and Christchurch were attended to by the tugs. The *Wendy Ann 2* (ex *C129*) was fitted with a special derrick over the stern and a diesel-driven winch to facilitate lifting the chains and sinkers, the buoys being towed into Poole for maintenance in rotation and replaced on station by another. The company had bought premises consisting of a store and office at West Quay Road, close to the Harbour in Poole. In the stores the crews made up the extra fendering and tow ropes for the tugs.

Sale of the tugs

By 1981 income was on the decline as ships became more manoeuvrable and work from the power station was rapidly decreasing. Ivor Holloway wanted to retire and the two remaining tugs were sold in July that year to the Poole Harbour Commissioners, the crews being taken on as employees of the Commissioners.

The tugs remained at Poole for some time longer. The *Wendy Ann II* was sold to Sutton Harbour Commissioners at Plymouth in 1984 to be replaced by the *Kingston Lacey* (ex *Kingston Buci* of Shoreham). The *Wendy Ann* lasted for another 12 years until 1996 when, with the imminent arrival of a brand new tug *Herbert Ballam* (the last vessel built at Bolson's yard), the last of Harry Rose's tugs finally left Poole at 19.00 on 12th June 1996, after sale to the Laxey Towing Company in the Isle of Man.

FLEET LIST

1. WENDY ANN 1947-1952 Wooden steam pinnace/motor tug

O.N. 182502 22gt 54.5 x 12.9 x 4.5 feet.
C.2-cyl. by McKie and Baxter Ltd., Paisley; 11 NHP.
1947: DH6-type oil engine by Gleniffer Engines Ltd., Glasgow; 120 BHP at 900 RPM.
1944: Built by James Silver, Rosneath for the Admiralty as a steam pinnace.
1947: Acquired by Harry Rose, Bournemouth and renamed WENDY ANN.
About 1952: Sold.

2. WENDY ANN 1950-1974 Steel tug

O.N. 185717 29gt 50.8 x 14.5 x 6.0 feet
5-cyl. oil engine by Mirrlees Blackstone; 200 BHP at 600 RPM with 2:1 reduction gearing. Bollard pull: 3 tons.
1950: Built by J. Bolson and Sons, Poole for Harry Rose, Bournemouth as WENDY ANN.
1974: Sold to Bain and Sons, Gravesend and renamed ANDREW II.

3. WENDY ANN II 1951-1957 Twin screw steel tender/tug

O.N. 149656 48g 14n 63.2 x 14.3 x 6.5 feet.
Two 4-cyl. 4T6 type semi-diesel engines by L. Gardner and Sons Ltd., Patricroft; each 96 BHP, 11.75 knots.
1951: Two 6-cyl. DH6 type oil engines by Gleniffer Engines Ltd., Glasgow; 120 BHP at 900 RPM with 2:1 reduction gearboxes. Bollard pull: 4 tons.
11.1.1928: Completed by W.J. Yarwood and Sons Ltd., Northwich (Yard No. 375) for the City of Liverpool (Port Health Authority), Liverpool as MOYLES.
24.5.1951: Acquired by Harry Rose, Bournemouth, renamed WENDY ANN II, subsequently rebuilt as a tug and re-engined.
6.1956. Register transferred to Poole.
1957: Sold to the British Dredging Works Co Ltd. (Eric E. Reade, manager), London and renamed CORUNNA.
7.1971: Sold to Irish owners and registry transferred to Dublin.

4. WENDY ANN III / WENDY ANN 2 1955-1981 Steel motor tug

O.N. 305371 44g 10n 63.2 x 15.51 x 8.0 feet
4-cyl. 4SCSA SS4M type oil engine by Petters Ltd., Loughborough; 250 BHP at 600 RPM; 9 knots.
3.1963: 4-cyl. 4ESSL type oil engine by Lister Blackstone Marine Ltd., Dursley; 400 BHP at 900 RPM with a Blackstone 3:1 gearbox; 11 knots. Bollard pull: 5 tons.
1940: Built by W.J. Yarwood and sons. Ltd., Northwich (Yard No. 646) for the Admiralty as C129.
17.2.1955: Acquired by Harry Rose, Bournemouth and renamed WENDY ANN III but not registered as such.
1963: Re-engined and registered at Poole as WENDY ANN 2 (although she had probably carried this name since 1957).
6.4.1964: Owners became Harry Rose (Towage) Ltd., Poole.
5.8.1981: Sold to Poole Harbour Commissioners, Poole.
5.12.1984: Sold to Sutton Harbour Commissioners, Plymouth.
1988: Sold to Western Ocean Towage Ltd. (S. Oates, manager), Plymouth.
1990: Sold to Captain N. Grenney, Plymouth.
Following main engine failure, sold to become houseboat at Southdown Quay, Millbrook Lake, Plymouth where still afloat (2003).

Wendy Ann II (ex Moyles) towing a timber ship. *[Poole Museums]*

5. VESPA/WENDY ANN 1969-1981
Steel tug

O.N. 163552 72g 6n 75.6 (82.0 o.l.)
x 18.5 x 9.0 feet

6-cyl. direct reversing oil engine by Mirrlees, Bickerton and Day Ltd., Stockport; 450 BHP.

1953: 7-cyl. M series direct reversing oil engine by British Polar Engines Ltd., Glasgow; 525 BHP.

1972: ESSL6 type oil engine by Mirrlees Blackstone Ltd., Stamford; 600 BHP at 900 RPM with Blackstone 3:1 reduction gearbox.

1934: Built by Alexander Hall, Aberdeen for Frederick Leyland Ltd., Liverpool as BRODSTONE.

1935: Sold to Blackfriars Lighterage, London and renamed EVELENE BRODSTONE.

1946: Sold to Gaselee and Son Ltd., London and renamed VESPA.

1953: Run down and sunk in Gallions Reach. Later raised, rebuilt and re-engined.

1965: Sold to Ship Towage (London) Ltd., London.

1969: Owners became London Tugs Ltd., London.

1969: Acquired by Harry Rose (Towage) Ltd., Poole.

1972: Rebuilt and re-engined at Husbands Shipyard, Marchwood.

1974: Renamed WENDY ANN and registered at Poole.

1981: Sold to Poole Harbour Commissioners, Poole.

1996: Sold to Laxey Towing Co Ltd., Douglas, Isle of Man.

10.2003: Still in service.

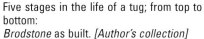

Five stages in the life of a tug; from top to bottom:

Brodstone as built. [Author's collection]

Vespa in Gaselee ownership. [Author's collection]

As *Wendy Ann* with *Wendy Ann 2* alongside at Poole Quay. [Author's collection]

Wendy Ann in Poole Harbour Commissioners ownership. [J. and M. Clarkson]

Wendy Ann in Douglas harbour when owned by Laxey Towing. [Author's collection]

A TRANSATLANTIC CAPTAIN AND HIS SHIPS
Charles Dawson

Captain Samuel Brooks was born in Todmorden, Yorkshire in 1831. The writer first heard about this unique man from his father who started his seafaring life in 1891 as the captain's servant in the *Arizona* of the Guion Line.

Samuel Brooks first went to sea as an apprentice in the schooner *Patriot* of Plymouth, engaged in the Mediterranean fruit trade. In 1851 and 1852 he sailed round Cape Horn to Panama and back in the brig *Bessie* of Liverpool, going out as able seaman and coming home, incredibly, in command. After certifying as first mate in Liverpool in 1853 he sailed to Calcutta in that capacity in the barque *Kedgeree* of Belfast.

With the Inman Line
After gaining his master's ticket in 1855, Samuel Brooks graduated to much larger vessels - and into steam - when he made his first voyage with the Inman Line as second mate of the *City of Baltimore*. She sailed from Liverpool for Marseilles on 20th March 1855 carrying troops for her

Captain Samuel Brooks, 1831-1904.
[Author's collection]

French charterer to the Mediterranean and Black Sea for service as a Crimean War transport. This was the beginning of his 26-year long connection with the line, during which he served in over a dozen of their ships. Duncan Haws once disclosed that they were early favourites of his: 'beautiful vessels, full of grace.' Inman's *City of Rome* of 1881 was, to this writer, about the most beautiful ship ever.

Originally named the Liverpool and Philadelphia Steam Ship Company, when it was founded in 1850, the Inman Line received its popular name as a compliment to William Inman, whose enthusiasm became the mainspring of the firm, and without which it may never have seen the light of day. As a clerk in the office of Richardson Brothers and Co. of Liverpool, he had been responsible for managing their fleet of sailing ships running between Liverpool and Philadelphia and in 1849, at 24 years of age, he was made a partner in the firm.

Although the *City of* prefix became bound up with the Inman Line, it was in fact the Glasgow shipbuilders Tod and McGregor who had introduced it. This was when they launched, presumably as a speculation, their iron screw steamer *City of Glasgow*, 1,609 gross tons, 227 x 34 feet, on 28th February 1850. Two months later, having no buyer, they placed her in service on their own account between Glasgow and New York. Inman, convinced of a sure future for steamships, watched her progress with great interest and, before the conclusion of her fourth voyage, persuaded his partners to buy her to run on their own route between Liverpool and Philadelphia, in competition with the company's sailing ships. The *City of Glasgow* commenced her inaugural voyage from Liverpool for Inman on 11th December 1850, under the command of Captain B.R. Matthews, formerly of the *Great Western*.

City of Manchester of 1851 was Inman's second ship. When sold in 1871, her engines were removed and she ran as a pure sailing ship until wrecked in 1876.   *[J. and M. Clarkson]*

Inman's second and third vessels were the *City of Manchester* and the *City of Philadelphia*. The *City of Baltimore* was their fourth and in 1856 Samuel Brooks was promoted to her first officer. She was now switched from war service and plied the route for Inman again from England to Philadelphia. Later that year, her port of call was re-scheduled to New York as part of the Inman policy to compete directly with the Cunard Line.

Cunard had established the first regular transatlantic passenger service and had gradually built up an impressive list of ever-increasing record speeds. But the competition was not only between lines but also between Britain and the US; it is significant that the year in which the US took the America's Cup, 1851, also saw the coveted Atlantic record go to the US-based Collins Line. But the losses of the *Arctic* in 1854 and the *Pacific* in 1856 were catastrophes from which Collins never really recovered and, after that, the honours returned to Cunard.

Samuel Brooks, remaining faithful to Inman, took command of the *Glasgow* on her first voyage for Inman at the end of 1859. She was another Tod and McGregor ship built in 1851 for the small, short-lived Glasgow and New York Steam Ship Company. Inman had bought her to replace the *City of Glasgow*, which was lost in 1854 without trace, with 480 casualties, a tragically record number at the time. The *Glasgow* herself was to be destroyed by fire at sea in 1865, fortunately without loss of life. Tragedy was to overcome Inman on a further occasion when the *City of Boston*, which Captain Brooks had commanded in 1866-7, disappeared without trace in 1870.

Was safety at sea sometimes sacrificed for speed? There was no doubt that, as representatives of their lines striving for supremacy on the high seas, captains must have been subjected to considerable pressure. The kudos to be attained by a 'Blue Riband' captain could only have been surpassed by that of the famous winners of the tea clipper premium races.

War had played a part in giving Captain Brooks promotion and it also contributed to Inman's success on the Atlantic. They had been quick to exploit the gap that the American Civil War had created: the *City of Brussels* had been the last of the three new *City* ships of increasing size that the line had ordered from Tod and McGregor in the attempt to win more trade, *City of Antwerp* and *City of Brooklyn* being the first two. With the success of the *City of Brussels,* the contest really opened out between the rival British lines. There was competition, not only for passengers, but also for the valuable mail contracts. Inman, for example, was awarded a mail subsidy in 1867, to replace the Cunard contract, which had been in operation since *Britannia's* days in 1840. In addition, in 1875, the *City of Berlin* gained the Blue Riband.

To Guion Line

After his 26 years with Inman, during which time he celebrated his 500th transatlantic crossing, in 1882 Captain Brooks joined one of the new contenders for the gleaming prizes to join the other rivals on the route: the Guion Line, founded in 1866. Perhaps he hoped for better fortune after the switch; his chances must have seemed bright when he was immediately given command of the famous *Arizona*. She had been designed expressly to capture the record and this she had done on her maiden voyage in 1879. She was staunch as well as swift for she survived ramming a giant iceberg at full speed off the Newfoundland Banks in November of that year, and was even able to make St. Johns under her own steam. After a new bow had been fitted, she beat her own record westward.

Captain Brooks had compensations for not immediately gaining the trophy with the *Arizona*. He was, after all, in charge of that type of vessel that came to be dubbed 'Atlantic Greyhound'. Now, after her initial burst, she had steadily become one of the most popular passenger ships in the trade, especially renowned for her superb comfort. This obviously reflected Guion policy, for already by April 1882, the new *Alaska* had taken over as record holder and in June of that year she broke through the bewitching seven-day barrier for the crossing.

In 1884, 'Harpers Monthly' wrote of the captain:

The largest North Atlantic liner when built in 1875, *City of Berlin* won the Blue Riband in that year. After sale to the USA in 1893, she became simply *Berlin,* and later the US Navy's transport and training ship *Meade,* surviving until 1921. *[J. and M. Clarkson]*

The *Arizona* of 1879 was built expressly to capture the Atlantic speed record for Guion Line. Seen here with her two funnels and four masts, but having lost some of her original yards, she was rebuilt for a Pacific service in 1894, and emerged with one very large funnel. As the US Navy transport *Hancock* she saw fitful service, mostly in wartime, but survived until 1927.   *[J. and M. Clarkson]*

'He is a man of powerful frame and distinguished appearance, who blends suavity with a dignity that never repels, but prevents intrusive familiarity. A host of people, known as well on one side of the sea as of the other, speak in terms of admiration of this popular officer'.

Captain Brooks served the last twelve years of his seafaring life in command of the *Arizona*. In 1888 he made his 600th transatlantic crossing with her. To celebrate this, a number of the captain's friends entertained him to dinner and presented him with an illuminated address in the glowing terms and florid style of the period. The tribute 'A faithful, trustworthy and skilful navigator' appears in that address. Its last sentence reads: 'May you be as prosperous as heretofore, and may no disaster to life or ship happen to mar so brilliant and successful a career'.

Captain Brooks lost neither ship nor passenger. However, it must have been a very sad day indeed for him when in October 1891 on the homeward run of *Arizona* he did lose a crew member, scullery man Walter Lanby, who was washed overboard in a strong westerly gale and never seen again.

On another voyage, in a dense fog at midnight, two days before arriving in New York, *Arizona* collided with a barque and appeared to have sunk her, since after cruising around searching for her, she could not be found. Later it was discovered that the barque, which had been carrying timber, had remained afloat. She was located some days after the collision and towed into Boston. The Guion Line eventually had to pay compensation to her owners.

Before these sad incidents, Captain Brooks had at least had the pleasure, in the autumn of 1891, of clipping two minutes from *Arizona*'s old eastbound record, but this was her last fling, especially as fresh financial troubles were brewing for the Guion Line. By 1893, the Guion fleet was sadly outdated and lasted only another year, until 1894. Another sign of the competitive times was that Inman had ceased operation the year before.

Captain Brooks must have been thankful to retire in June 1894, after nearly fifty years of service at sea. He had by then amassed the incredible figure of 690 transatlantic crossings. The sheets listing his voyages in the Board of Trade BT 122 records from 1851 to 1894 are so packed with names and dates, that they almost have the appearance of a full orchestral score. In December 1894 Captain Brooks won the then handsome prize of £10 offered by the weekly paper 'Titbits' to the sailor who could prove that he had travelled the greatest number of miles on the ocean. His over two million miles, which the writer was fortunately able to have quoted in the 'Guinness Book of Records' in 1978, stands as a wonderful achievement.

His Inman ships and the dates of his years or part years in command of them are listed below.

City of Baltimore	1855-7 and 1863
Kangaroo	1857-60
City of Manchester	1858-9
Glasgow	1859
Edinburgh	1860-1
City of Washington	1861-6
Etna	1862-3
City of Boston	1866-7
City of London	1867-9
City of Brooklyn	1869-71
City of Brussels	1872-3 and 1880
City of Antwerp	1873
City of Richmond	1873-6
City of Montreal	1877-8
City of Chester	1878-81

Note that ships without the *City of* prefix retained their names from their previous owners, from whom Inman bought them: *Kangaroo* from the Australasian Pacific Mail Steam Packet Co.; *Glasgow* and *Edinburgh* from the Glasgow and New York Steam Ship Company and *Etna* from Cunard.

Captain Brooks enjoyed some ten years of retirement in his hometown where he died and was buried in 1904.

Although ships' speeds have increased enormously and conditions on board have improved beyond all recognition since Captain Brooks' days, the tenacity and sense of duty of men like him is unlikely ever to be matched. No man would now stick it that long. They certainly bred them tough in those days.

City of Montreal of 1872 was built by the Inman Line to compete with White Star vessels. With a simple steam engine, she was technologically rather backward and was uneconomic. In 1876 she was fitted with a compound engine, apparently gaining a second funnel, as seen here. In August 1887 a fire took hold in her cotton cargo and she burnt out in the Atlantic, although fortunately all passengers and crew were rescued.
[J. and M. Clarkson]

Inman Line's next ship after *City of Montreal,* the Caird-built *City of Chester* of 1873, had compound engines from new. She was another Inman ship that passed to the American Line, becoming simply *Chester* in 1893. Like *Berlin* she was taken up for use as a transport during the Spanish-American War of 1898, being renamed *Sedgwick*. Italian owners then had a few years use from her as *Arizona* and later *Neapole-tano* until broken up in 1907.
[J. and M. Clarkson]

Experience with *City of Montreal* led her Clydeside builders, Tod and MacGregor, to incorporate improvements in *City of Richmond* of 1873, including compound engines and two funnels to increase draft to her boilers. She was sold in 1891 and broken up, still as *City of Richmond* but now Norwegian, in 1896.
[J. and M. Clarkson]

IRON LADIES FOLLOW UP

John Harrison's three articles on BISCO ore carriers have enjoyed wide acclaim, stimulating considerable correspondence but commendably few corrections. Additional information received is presented below.

Maipo and *Knightsgarth:* ships that go bump in the dock
In the first part of his trilogy, John Harrison referred to a collision in Birkenhead Docks on 2nd November 1973. Although not quite witnessing the event, Paul Boot was on the scene soon afterwards and provides a commentary on the incident, and dramatic photographs of its aftermath.

Knightsgarth had arrived not long before from Point Central and, unusually, was laying by at the far end of Cavendish Wharf on the south side of the West Float, awaiting a berth in Bidston Dock to discharge her cargo of iron ore. On the north side of the dock, and some way astern, the steam-turbine powered *Maipo* (10,869/1966) was near to completing loading for South America on the berth that had been used for many years by the Bibby and Henderson Lines services. Located at the end of the dock, where the Duke Street passage divides the meandering East and West Floats, the quay is angled towards Cavendish Wharf.

During the late afternoon of what had been a dismal autumn day, I passed through the docks and in the gloom noticed the *Maipo* skewed across the dock with numerous tugs in attendance. At the end of the quay, where she had been tied up, the frayed ends of several mooring ropes still attached to the bollards indicated a sudden and uncontrolled departure. *Maipo* had reportedly been turning her engines - presumably either to warm through the turbines or perhaps to test the machinery after repairs. Although it seemed that extra lines had been put out these were obviously not sufficient to resist the thrust against the quay wall close to the stern. Steam turbines are not noted for their rapid response to manoeuvres at the best of times and it may well have taken a short while before anyone realised what had happened and was able to react to the situation. In the 1,000 feet or so that separated the two ships, *Maipo* had built up sufficient momentum to embed herself in the starboard side of the *Knightsgarth*, missing the accommodation block by less than a 100 feet. Later in the evening as attempts to separate the two ships continued, I returned in the hope of taking some photographs. Thanks to the police officer in attendance, who obtained permission for me from the captain, I was able to go on board the *Knightsgarth* and had a grandstand view of the proceedings. Although the damage may not look particularly severe at deck level, the full bulbous bow of the *Maipo* had penetrated deep into the hull of *Knightsgarth,* tearing through the shell plating from the deck right down to the bottom plates. After cutting away the impacted steelwork, the two ships were finally separated during the night with the assistance of the tugs. Fortunately a dry dock was available within the West Float and *Knightsgarth* was able to sail little less than three weeks later after repairs had been completed.

On a distantly related matter, could I add a footnote to Peter Myers's letter in *Record* 24. Not only have the gantry unloaders disappeared from the Bidston ore quay but so too has the dock itself which was completely infilled during 2002.

Grid locked
A.D. Frost of Sunderland made his first trip to sea in the ore carrier *Silvercrag,* sailing from Middlesbrough in November 1968 to load at Murmansk. At the latter port steel grids were put over the hatches and iron ore dropped in from bridge height out of grabs. When he asked why they did this, he was told it was to deter would-be Russian tourists going to the UK.

Further to 'Iron Colours' in *Record* 24, Mr Frost notes that the owner of *Silvercrag,* St. Helens Shipping Co. Ltd., changed its funnel colours similarly to Bishopsgate Shipping Co. Ltd., but without the 'B' alongside the houseflag panel. Close study of the photograph of the same company's *Silversand* on page 29 of *Record* 25 shows she carries these funnel colours.

South Wales owners and ore carriers
David Jenkins was intrigued that only Gibbs of the South Welsh shipowners invested in ore carriers, despite their trading to local ports. David's investigations suggest local shipowners such as Reardon Smith, Graig Shipping and Walter Gould were not convinced that the BISCO charters offered sufficiently attractive remuneration. Gould, for instance, had two Empire types, *Grelmarion* and *Grelrosa,* enjoying excellent freight rates in the mid 1950s. Come the post-Suez slump, however, and freight rates slumped. Gould, for instance, was forced to sell up at the end of the decade. Perhaps owning BISCO ore carriers would have helped them survive.

Campbells
David Burrell offers information on the shipowning Campbells of Glasgow and Newcastle, who came from New Cumnock. In the 1920s they built ore carriers to serve the Baird iron interests in Scotland. *Dalhanna's* owners were Northern Mercantile and Investment Corporation Ltd., a Baird company. When their Spanish ore mines closed they opened up in Sierra Leone and owned 95% of the Sierra Leone Development Co. Later Baird changed entirely, from heavy industry into the rag trade. They famously lost their Marks and Spencers contracts some years ago.

The Houlder ore carriers
John B. Hill knew Houlder's ore carriers well. Commenting on the caption to the lower photo on page 213, although he deserved it John M. Houlder was said to have turned down a knighthood, settling for an O.B.E. and so was not plain Mr John Houlder. Now in his eighties, John Houlder is still active in shipping circles and a director of the Hadley Shipping Co. Ltd. He used to relate that the names of Houlder's ore carriers were chosen by himself and his wife, also that they had no specific meanings.

John Houlder was much involved in the design of the six small ore-carriers and John believes that credit should be given to him for the all-aft superstructure. This was an innovation, later adopted by other owners and now universally accepted in all bulk carriers and tankers. It must have proved a big benefit to those involved in loading and discharging the ships, although there were initially some raised eyebrows amongst the captains, who were not accustomed to conning their ships from so far aft!

Two views of *Maipo's* bows embedded in *Knightsgarth's* hull, 2nd November 1973. *[Paul Boot]*

As they had decided to have the ships diesel propelled, Houlders had no alternative but to accept the two, five-cylinder geared Gray-Polar propulsion arrangement for the first four ships, because of delivery constraints. William Gray's Central Marine Engine Works did not have a licence to build Doxford engines at the time but, in the case of the *Oregis* and *Oremina*, Hawthorn, Leslie's St. Peter's Works were able to supply five-cylinder engines of the Doxford type. The Central Marine Engine Works built their first Doxford engine in 1959 and were thus in a position to provide Doxford engines when the *Mabel Warwick* and *Joya*

McCance were built the following year.

The Gray-Polar engines were not as reliable as the slow speed Doxford engines, particularly the ring-piston scavenge blowers, but were kept running by hard work on the part of the ships' engineers. It was not unusual for maintenance to occupy most of the short spells in port, the engineers preferred this to overhauling one engine at sea, as suggested by John Harrison, although it could be done in an emergency. It is no exaggeration to say that the Doxford engines required less than half the man-hours for maintenance, compared with the Gray-Polar machinery, hence the popularity of the former type amongst the ships' engineers.

The accompanying account of life on board the Houlder ore carriers by Captain A. Fowler was written at the behest of John Hill. Captain Fowler joined Houlder Brothers from the Royal Navy in 1946 and was promoted master in 1960. He retired in 1988 and died about three years ago. Small in stature, but very lively, Captain Fowler was liked by all who sailed with him and his notes modestly describe what could be a hard, uncomfortable life, particularly in northern waters in winter.

Life on the ore carriers: Captain Fowler's story

My service on Houlder's ore carrier started with my first command on *Oreosa* in 1956, and over the next ten years I had command of all but two of the Houlder ships, namely *Orepton* and *Mabel Warwick*. I went round the fleet twice as we had six months' duty, this sometimes extending to seven or eight months, before we were relieved for leave. My last ship was the *Joya McCance*.

The story goes that John Houlder went to Port Talbot with a tape measure to measure the width of the lock, and then built his ships with about six inches to spare on each side. They were all built at William Gray's West Hartlepool shipyard.

We traded to many places: Pepel and Takoradi in West Africa; the Mediterranean ports of Almeria, Mellila, Bone, Bougie, Algiers, Tunis (La Goulette); Poti, a Black Sea port in Russia; Narvik; Lulea; Seven Islands (Sept Isles) in the St Lawrence river; Wabana in Newfoundland; and Brazil. In Great Britain our main ports of discharge were Port Talbot, Birkenhead, Workington, Barrow-in-Furness, Glasgow, Middlesbrough, and occasionally the Ford car works at Dagenham. In Port Talbot the use of grabs made discharge very rapid, usually about 12 hours, and we had to clear the berth as soon as the last grab went over the side and go to a lay-by to await the tide. And in some ports such as Narvik loading could be almost as quick: and I well remember loading 9,000 tons in two and a half hours in Sept Isles and not even seeing the port because we went in through thick fog on radar and left in the dark just a few hours later.

It was good to get a Mediterranean port where loading was slow. And occasionally, welcoming the sight of two or three ships ahead of us, we enjoyed a good night's sleep in ports like Workington or Birkenhead. Because we got so little time in port to rest, especially in winter, the work was hard. Going to Narvik in winter was the most uncomfortable. Storm force winds and constant heavy rolling meant that it was difficult to stand on one's feet and this was very tiring. After two or three voyages within the Arctic Circle in the middle of winter, it was wonderful to be sent to a Mediterranean port or to West Africa and sail along quietly in smooth waters.

This page and opposite: Houlder's *Oregis* and the tug *Northsider* aground at Tynemouth in March 1974. See *Record* 25, page 24.

[Malcolm Donnelly]

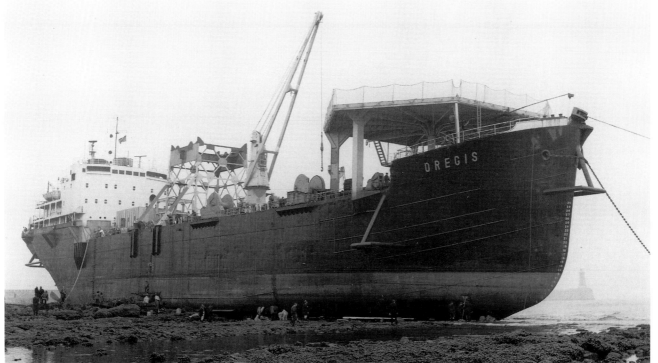

Occasionally in Port Talbot or Workington we were neaped and had to wait for the spring tides. At Port Talbot this meant anchoring in Swansea Bay which was fine in the summer but in the winter storms in the Bristol Channel the ship was liable to drag her anchor and we had to seek shelter. Some masters preferred to go under Lundy Island, but I did not take kindly to creeping under Lundy with gale force winds howling over the cliff tops. My choice was Barnstaple Bay. The entrance to Port Talbot was narrow and tricky but the pilots there were very skilled. As there was only two feet of water under the keel at the entrance, entry had to be made at the top of high water. The *Orelia* ran aground there in the early days, but was refloated at the next high water with the aid of tugs and without damage. I understand that the folk from Aberavon and Port Talbot got quite a thrill from walking round the ship at low water. Not so the master and senior officers, who would have been very worried.

The accommodation on board all the ships was of a very high standard, with all officers and crew members having single-berth cabins, and the ships were well manned for their size. Most of the crew of around 40 came from the Port Talbot area and from other South Wales ports. A few were from the North East coast. Most were reliable, and for the local men it was a good job as they usually got a night in port to visit their families after about three weeks at sea. Our longest voyage - to Brazil and back - was about six weeks. Some of the engineer officers were from West Hartlepool and had served their apprenticeships in Gray's, the shipbuilder's yard.

The engines in *Oreosa*, *Orelia*, *Oredian* and *Orepton* were of Swedish design, with the two engines geared to one shaft. The Doxfords engines, which were fitted in the *Oregis*, *Oremina*, *Mabel Warwick*, and *Joya McCance* and proved more reliable, had not been available for the four earlier ships. The pistons on all the ships had to be lifted, cleaned and overhauled at frequent intervals, and this heavy work was undertaken during a short stay in port. Often it was an all-night job. Most of the repairs were carried out by the ship's engineers with occasional help from Port Talbot Dry Dock Company. Dry docking was usually every twelve months at the Port Talbot Dry Dock, and included scrubbing and painting the ship's bottom.

The ships were popular with the crews. Usually quite a large amount of overtime was allowed and worked to keep the ship to a high standard of cleanliness and efficiency. They were well-painted, smart ships and we took great pride in their appearance. On the North Atlantic and Narvik voyages they got rather weather worn, but the damage was made good on the fine weather voyages. In heavy weather the decks were always awash and at times it was like being on a half-submerged submarine. An enormous amount of water was shipped, but ran off quickly through the side ports and guard rails. In hazardous times lifelines were rigged on the fore deck to enable the crew to move along the deck to the forward store-rooms.

All four holds were fitted with Macgregor steel hatch covers to keep them watertight. Water ballast was carried in eight wing tanks which had to be pumped out before and during the loading operations. These ballasting arrangements were very good and the ships could be well down in the water on the outward passages. Fresh water for drinking, cooking and bathing was a problem at times. There were only two 40-ton tanks to serve a crew of 40 for up to three weeks, and water had sometimes to be rationed, especially if the ship was likely to be neaped at Port Talbot as there was no water available there. The two larger ships did have a desalination system on board which helped matters.

The ships were well served by the management and local agencies. Our agent in Port Talbot, Willie Evans, would always cycle down to meet ship on her arrival, in the middle of the night if necessary. He carried the crew's wages, between £2,000 and £3,000, in a carrier bag on his handlebars. Those were trusting times. Latterly in home ports the agency was taken over by James Fisher in Barrow and by the British Iron and Steel Corporation. Before arrival we radioed in for crew replacements, cash, stores and fuel requirements as all these operations had to be undertaken whilst we were discharging. The foreign agencies were usually provided by the ore company which was loading the ship.

We always loaded a full cargo of iron ore, about 9,000 tons (or 15,000 tons for the two large vessels) and this would put the ship down to her marks. There were summer and winter load lines, depending on the season.

Swedish ore, which was shipped in Narvik and other northern ports, was heavy and peaked at the bottom of each hold, thereby increasing the rolling on the homeward passage. In contrast the Mediterranean and West African ores were lighter and nearly filled the holds to capacity, but they were very dusty and during loading operations the ship was enveloped in the a cloud of ore dust. We had to keep the portholes and doors leading to the open deck firmly closed. High-pressure hoses quickly cleared the decks from dust once loading was complete.

As seamen we were rather dubious about the handling capabilities in narrow waters of these ore carriers because the bridge was so much further from the bows than in conventional ships. However, we soon became accustomed to the change in line of sight. At sea the high superstructure aft acted as a sail and steadied the ship when she was hove to in heavy weather with the wind and the sea on either bow. Very little water was shipped under these conditions and the ships rode comfortably in gale force winds. However, in narrow waters and a strong beam wind the steering had to be watched carefully.

Location, location, location

To finish, a letter from Martyn Morgan of Cardiff which expresses appreciation of John Harrison's efforts and identifies some of the locations of photographs.

Grateful thanks to Mr. Harrison, and to your superb journal for the recent features on the 'Iron Ladies'. These fine, robust, perhaps unglamorous and somewhat overlooked ships have finally received the recognition and appreciation they deserve. These vessels were frequent visitors to my city, their cargoes destined for the now non-existent East Moors Steelworks. Discharge would be in Roath Dock, and on average took three days.

Page 238 of *Record* 24: *Cape Howe* has just left the Queen Alexandra Lock at Cardiff, as has *Dunkyle* on page 240.

Page 239: *Mabel Warwick* is about to enter the same lock on a fine summer's morning, whilst also on page 239, *Sagamore* is awaiting discharge.

Page 240: *Dunadd* has been discharged, but for some reason is lying at P. Leiner's Wharf in Roath Dock.

MORE DAYS MORE DOLLARS - TWO TESTING VOYAGES

Tony Westmore

When signing on for a voyage a sailor never knew quite how long he would be away, or sometimes where his discharge port would be, particularly if he were signing on a sailing vessel. Usually seamen would be offered a straight monthly or weekly wage or, if one voyage to a known destination was involved, perhaps a rate for the job. If a choice were offered the decision obviously had to be thought through.

The last British full-rigged ship

The *William Mitchell* was destined to be the last of her kind, a full-rigged ship employed in worldwide trading under the British flag, with London on her stern. In 1920 she was voyaging the globe seeking any cargo available. At this time the high freights resulting from the First World War were still available - but only just, time was running out and by the following year life for the deep-water commercial sailing vessel would become very difficult. The *William Mitchell* was built by W.J. Bigger in Londonderry and launched in 1892.

She was built as a full rigger for the Belfast Foyle Line, named after a local councillor, and of 1,885gt. She surprisingly retained her full rig throughout, why I am not sure, as this must have increased her running expenses later through crew manning numbers. In 1909 she was purchased by John Stewart and Company, in whose fleet she was to remain until her end. Although she gave good service, she is better remembered by her longer passages together with her other

troubles, which rather overshadowed her good passages.

Towards the end of September 1920, the *William Mitchell* had almost completed loading timber at Gulfport in the Mississippi Sound, when a hurricane warning was given for the area, so that precautionary extra moorings were speedily arranged. In spite of the efforts taken, the US four-masted wooden barqentine *Amazon*, moored just ahead of the *William Mitchell*, was carried away from her moorings and swung around on to the stem of the ship and ran along her side causing considerable damage, the *William Mitchell's* bowsprit bringing down her jigger mast in the process. The *Amazon* later cleared away and lay at anchor for the remainder of the night. Next morning the damage to the *William Mitchell* was assessed and found to consist of a buckled bobstay and a jib-boom guy carried away, plus damage to plates, davits, rails and stanchions. Making good the damage was to occupy another week, and prior to her being able to sail she was also in need of extra crew members, as eight able seamen had left at Gulfport - no doubt to take advantage of the higher rates of pay offered in the States. The Captain offered the new men 400 dollars for the voyage down to Buenos Aires, informing them that he expected the voyage to take about 60 days, but surprisingly they opted for a rate of 100 dollars a month (the local going rate). The Captain's estimate of a 60-day voyage was perhaps a little optimistic. Seventeen sailing ships had sailed from Gulfport for the River Plate during the thirteen months up to February

William Mitchell at a British port, possibly in South Wales. *[World Ship Photo Library]*

Two views of *William Mitchell* under sail. *[Monterey Museum]*

1921. For these the average voyage was 92 days, all of the ships taking between 62 and 144 days.

Of the eight new recruits, four reportedly had no previous seagoing time, whilst only two had any previous sail experience. This was a condition that was becoming more difficult to satisfy among sailing ship operators - invariably it was the apprentices who were manning what remained of the British sailing fleet, the *William Mitchell* having twelve apprentices aboard at this time.

With her new recruits, she was able to clear Gulfport under tow on 6th October 1920, bound at last for Buenos Aires with timber loaded both in the hold and as deck cargo. It was over a fortnight before the Florida Straits were passed, and she continued making easting, but later became becalmed for several weeks. Eventually the Equatorial Current took hold of the ship setting her in towards the Brazilian coast.

On 26th December land was sighted, it later becoming evident that it extended a considerable way around the vessel. As a breeze sprang up she was put on to the other tack and managed to clear the land, as the wind failed the current again took hold of her, and by the end of January there was still no improvement in her position - not having yet weathered Cape San Roque and furthermore both provisions and water were becoming very short.

A steamer was sighted, but attempts at signalling to attract attention seeking extra provisions proved to be of no avail. By the 14th February she had again set in to the land. Managing to get clear of the coast, the Captain decided on putting the ship on a heading for Barbados, a course that she held more successfully, and she eventually arrived there on 2nd March 1921, after being 147 days at sea.

Just prior to this, concern for the ship's safety was being raised both by Lloyds in London and their agents in Buenos Aires and, as no reports of her had been received, she was being quoted on the re-insurance market at 60 guineas per cent. At Barbados four days were spent taking on stores and water supplies - sufficient for two months. She again set sail on 6th March, six months after her departure from Gulfport, and headed out north-eastward, planning to make enough easting to weather Cape San Roque, before heading south. The line was crossed on 27th March in 23 degrees 30 minutes west. A south westerly gale was encountered on 2nd June and she remained hove to for about three days, at this time the food supplies again caused concern, food rationing having to resume. Following the gale, light airs and calms persisted for another ten days,

before another gale in the form of a violent pampero took its toll, during which several sails were lost, together with a considerable amount of her deck cargo, which had broken adrift. The wind now held fair and Lobos Island was encountered on 24th June where the pilot boarded. All was still not well, however, for strong unfavourable winds forced her to anchor for a couple of days, before kinder winds enabled her to arrive at Buenos Aires on 27th June 1921, 266 days out of Gulfport. This is thought to have been the longest voyage by a vessel of John Stewart and Company. At Buenos Aires she subsequently loaded a cargo of linseed for Falmouth, her orders then taking her on to Ipswich.

The last British square rigger built

By a strange coincidence the crew of another British sailing vessel of some distinction were being similarly frustrated on a voyage south to Australia at the same time as, and within the vicinity of, the *William Mitchell*. The four-masted barque *Archibald Russell* was popularly thought of as being the last square rigger to be built for British owners. Built by Scott's Shipbuilding and Engineering Co. Ltd. at Greenock in 1905 for John Hardie and Company of Glasgow, she was named after a close business friend of his and was of 2,354gt. On 30th October 1920 she had sailed from Terneuzen under tow, bound towards Melbourne. She soon faced a south westerly gale in the Channel with her tug struggling to keep her off the Goodwins. Having cleared the sands, the tug and tow were then unable to clear Dungeness, and an anchorage was taken, with further assistance being sought in the form of another tug. The *Archibald Russell* was then towed to safety but, while the anchors were being hove up, one of them became obstructed and, before being able to part the cable, the windlass became damaged, proving to be beyond the capabilities of the crew to repair. She was subsequently towed to the Solent and anchored off Cowes on 2nd November 1920 to enable the damage to be made good. Repairs took 18 days to complete, and on 20th November she set sail again for Melbourne. Nothing was subsequently heard or reported of her until 81 days later, when she anchored off St. Vincent in the Cape Verde Islands. At this stage it could have been expected that she would be well on her way to, if not nearing, Australian waters. On reporting to her owners, she enquired concerning other cargo availability, but she was again instructed to proceed for Melbourne: apparently she was still adequately stocked. She sailed again on 14th February 1921, and some 100 days later approached the coast of

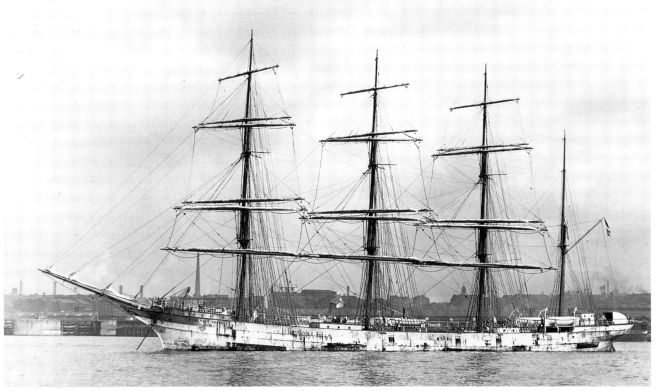

A weather-beaten *Archibald Russell,* photographed by Basil Feilden at anchor in the Mersey. *[J. and M. Clarkson collection]*

Archibald Russell in light airs with all sails set. *[Amos and Amos, Dover; courtesy of World Ship Photo Library]*

Australia, not surprisingly beginning to experience shortages of food, cigarettes and tobacco. Fortunately she was able to restock her stores with help from a passing steamer and eventually made Melbourne, 205 days out of Terneuzen.

Long voyages like these two would have been a severe test for all on board, as the crew would have to work harder in getting nowhere, continually bracing the yards attempting to make the most of each subtle change of wind, and on completion of one order the wind would invariably move to another quarter. Added to this the *William Mitchell* was a notoriously heavy ship to work. With these facts plus the rations of both food and fags, tempers must have become very frayed. This area off the Brazilian coast could prove hazardous for any skipper who ventured too close to the land as, on losing the wind, the strong westerly-setting equatorial current would sweep them towards the coast .

Subsequent to these two voyages similar fates befell these vessels, both being laid up on their return to home waters, as did many of the other remaining deep water commercial sailing vessels at this time, many of the ports around Europe being occupied by them on their return from foreign waters. With profitable employment becoming hard to find, it was generally considered better to lay up ships than run them at a loss.

The *William Mitchell*, after laying up at Gravesend for just under two years, was to return to service, more perhaps to satisfy her owners' passion of providing apprentices an opportunity of sail experience, than as a means of financial return. She really did neither herself nor her operators any favours with some extended passages and several costly

incidents during her few remaining years. The *William Mitchell* sailed from Tocopilla with her final cargo on 30th August 1927, the last bag of nitrate having been shantied aboard, in an attempt to repeat what had happened on so many previous occasions at these ports. Alas, she was the only sailing vessel there, the steamers not responding in the time-honoured fashion of the ships bell or echoing cheers of their sailing predecessors, thus she was the last sailing vessel to raise the Southern Cross on the west coast of South America. On this voyage she transited the Panama Canal, arriving at Ostend on 25th November 1927. She was subsequently sold to Belgium shipbreakers and broken up the following year. Her disposal brought to an end the sailing ship fleet of John Stewart and Company.

The *Archibald Russell,* on her return to home waters in December 1921, discharged her grain at Cardiff and a period of idleness followed until she was sent to lay up at Milford Haven, and offered for sale. It was here in 1923 that she was fortunate to came to the attention of possibly the only person who could offer a sailing vessel any form of future at this time, the Aland Islander Gustaf Erikson. He later acquired her together with two other vessels of the John Hardie fleet, the *Hougomont* and *Killoran*. He was able to obtain some profitable service out of the *Archibald Russell* up until the Second World War, when she was to remain in British waters at Goole. She was later taken over by the British for use as a stores ship and returned to Erikson in 1946, though she remained idle, having been stripped down to her lower masts. On Erikson's death in 1947 she was put up for sale, and subsequently sold for breaking up by J.J. King at Gateshead. Their like will never be seen again.

Opposite upper: Seen at anchor in the Mersey whilst still under British ownership, the Ailsa-built *Killoran* (1,817/1900) was another Hardie square rigger which ended her days with Gustaf Erikson of Mariehamn. On 10th August

1940 she was captured in the Atlantic by the German auxiliary *Widder* and sunk by explosive charges. *[J. and M. Clarkson]*

Opposite lower: A near-sister to the *Archibald Russell,* the Scotts-built four-

masted barque *Hougomont* (2,378/1897) was sold to Gustav Erikson in 1925. After being sold in damaged condition in 1932, she was dismantled for use as a breakwater in Australia. *[NMM P3749]*

PUTTING THE RECORD STRAIGHT

Letters, additions, amendments and photographs relating to articles in any issues of *Record* are welcomed. Letters may be lightly edited. E-mails are welcome, but senders are asked to include their postal address.

A stern in the engine room

Many thanks for your Ships in Focus *Record* 24. Once again the quality and diversity of the articles is first class.

With reference to the photo feature 'Old Wine - New Bottles' I found it very interesting, particularly regarding the *City of Capetown* which had been built at Alexander Stephen and Sons, Linthouse Shipyard in 1959 as ship number 651, the *City of Melbourne.*

As she was building, I was a pre-apprentice with Stephens, just about to commence my five-year electrician's apprenticeship. The main engine mentioned in your article was, at the time, the largest Sulzer ever constructed in Britain and many of the technical press visited Stephen's engine works to see the shop trials before the engine was dismantled and moved to the berth for shipping. The engine in its complete state weighed over 680 tons.

The practice by Stephens at that time, was to complete the hull and prepare the engine room for shipping of auxiliaries, bedplate and as much of the engine as possible before launch on their ships. Sometimes the funnel would also be shipped. This depended on the berth craneage and number of decks above the main deck. On some vessels shipping of heavier items were completed at the fitting-out quay at Shieldhall Wharf.

At the same time as ship 651 (*City of Melbourne*) was building, ship 663 the *Risdon* (4,125/1959) was being constructed for the Union Steamship Company of New Zealand, a much smaller ship. As the engine room of the *City of Melbourne* was being prepared for the shipping of equipment - staging was cleared round the engine casing to allow unrestricted access - the stern unit of the *Risdon* was completing in the Fabrication Shed.

When it was completed, the *Risdon's* stern was transported to the berth and then had to be swung over the *City of Melbourne* by two of the berth cranes to reach its position on the adjacent berth. Just as the unit was passing over the engine room of the *City of Melbourne,* the rigging assembly failed and the stern unit of the *Risdon* fell neatly into the engine room of the *City of Melbourne.* Luckily no-one was injured by the unit failing, although a caulker was trapped for hours in the engine room double bottom until they could get access to him because the manhole had been covered over by the failing unit. It took many days and not a few unprintable words to get the *Risdon's* stern out of 651's engine room.

I enclose an aerial view of the *City of Melbourne* on speed trials on the Arran Mile; it gives another perspective of this classic cargo liner. The famous Glasgow photographers of William Ralston and Sons, who were ship photographers for many of the Clyde yards, took this photo. Photography was also used as proof when shipbuilders submitted a claim for payment to the shipowner. Typical instalments were Order Placed, Keel Laid, 25%, 50%, 75% Erection on the Berth, Launch and Delivery. Ralstons took photos of progress of each hull and these photos along with a tonnage erected sheet signed by the shipyard director were then sent to the owner in the hope that he would cough up the payment. Using this system meant that most shipyards had large overdrafts with the banks because of the materials they had to purchase up front, so reaching an instalment milestone was most welcome.

From 1946 until their closure in 1970, Stephens used photography to record the construction of all its ships. The Shipyard Planning Department was responsible for keeping a photo album of each ship showing the erection tonnage achieved and they gave a fascinating insight into seeing lumps of metal turn into ships, launching and sailing away for world wide trading.

When ordered, *City of Melbourne* was to have been a sister to ship 650 *City of Newcastle,* which had been launched in 1956. However, the option of trying out this new and much more powerful Sulzer was taken up by Ellerman Lines and the *City of Melbourne* became a one-off.

WILLIAM RIDDELL, 6 Hunter Drive, Stonehaven, Aberdeenshire AB39 2BG.

More on *Magdalena*

At the time of the loss of Royal Mail's *Magdalena* (April 1949) Blue Funnel were having *Helenus* (10,125/1949) and *Hector* (10,125/1950) built at Belfast. I remember the late Stopford Holt (youngest son of Lawrence D. Holt - Alfred Holt's senior partner) coming back from a launching ceremony saying that there was anxiety at Harland and Wolff over possible structural weakness in *Magdalena's* design where she broke her back.

In the area of forward frames 15 to 20 there were a pair of public rooms for passengers which had recessed wells over them, namely the lounge at boat deck level with an observation lounge above; the first class dining saloon (on the shelter deck) with a recess over it (at bridge deck level) and only the smoke room (promenade deck) sandwiched in between. The haunting photo of *Magdalena* ashore in Imbui Bay, at the approaches to Rio de Janeiro, clearly shows the features of the structure of the ship that was being worried over by the builders.

When the trio of As were built (1959-1960) none of the possible mistakes in *Magdalena's* design were repeated in the layout of the 'Three Graces'.

David Burrell says that the builder's scale model of *Magdalena* was removed from Royal Mail's City of London head office soon after the wreck and its fate has never been established.
ANDREW BELL, Gartul, Porthleven, Helston, Cornwall TR13 9JJ

The *Magdalena* story is a relatively unknown (and thus interesting) but tragic one. She was indeed built to replace the October 1940 war loss *Highland Patriot,* but there were only four (not five) surviving *Highlands* after the Second World War. The *Highland Patriot* was built to replace the *Highland Hope* (wrecked in 1930), and the survivors were the *Highland Monarch, Chieftain, Brigade* and *Princess*.

There is also mention of the 'Cagarras Reefs' as the place where the *Magdalena* came to grief - perhaps the Tijucas Rocks form part of a larger area. The ship's turbines were salvaged and used in a power station at Manaos for many years. Some lifeboats were used to equip other Royal Mail newbuildings. Attempts to tow the stern portion off the beach were abandoned, and it was sold to Brazilian buyers for breaking up piecemeal in situ. The forepart was blown up as it constituted a danger to navigation. I wonder if the £50,000 figure mentioned by Mr Bower included the proceeds of the salvaged turbines?

I was trying to reconcile the fact that all passengers were taken off safely with his father's saving himself by swimming, but I suppose Mr Bower Senior's escape occurred the following day when the ship broke apart.
ROBERT H. LANGLOIS, Feu Follet, Maisons au Comte Road, Vale, Guernsey GY3 51H

As one of the declining number of ship enthusiasts who have actually seen the ill-fated liner *Magdalena*, observed loading in the Royal Docks, I read the article with some interest.

Can I point out that the phrase 'being designed to run with the five surviving ex Nelson Line motorships', is incorrect as only four of these vessels existed in 1949. Five sisters were originally built, including *Highland Hope* (14,129/1930) wrecked on the Farilhoes 19th November 1930, almost brand new. Her replacement *Highland Patriot* (14,172/1932) brought the fleet up to the required number for eight years, until her loss to *U 38* on 1st October 1940, and *Magdalena* fared even worse. The quartermasters on watch at the time of the mishap were not held liable, but were invited to seek a berth elsewhere, and shared the bridge watches in *Llangibby Castle* (12,044/1929) during my first year at sea.

Another of 'my' ships is to be found in the Canadian Pacific article, the *Beaverglen* in which I made six UK to Canada voyages during 1958. It is appropriate to see her funnel emitting the inevitable cloud of black smoke, as these ships were absolutely filthy aft of the accommodation block. When proceeding aft to join the second mate's mooring party, the hands could all be heard chorusing the 'Beaver song', 'Smoke gets in your eyes'!

The sooty deposit covering the decks sounded like a walk through a layer of incinerated cornflakes, making these heavy-working ships difficult to keep clean. Paintwork was also a real problem on the North Atlantic run, and along with the paint pot and brush, a large handful of cotton waste was used with some vigour to wipe the surface clear of spray before a liberal coat of mast colour was applied. As one would expect, the trapped moisture caused the paint to lift, and several previous layers also, which looked remarkably like book pages flapping in the wind!
ALAN PHIPPS, 2 Riverside Road, Droitwich Spa, Worcestershire WR9 8UW

At Beauty Point

On going through *Record* 24 page 228 the photo of the *Otagold* ex *City of Capetown* made me look through my photos at Beauty Point, Port Dalrymple, Tasmania. I have a photo of *Otagold* alongside to load a cargo of apples and pears for Singapore. She sailed for Singapore from here on the 23rd April 1979 for what was her last cargo-carrying voyage. I have this information as I worked as a shipwright and then in a clerical capacity on the wharves here.

The photo above her of the *Bulima* was interesting as she was another caller to Beauty Point for fruit and drums of tallow for the east.

One photo I have is of the *Port Alfred* sailing from here with a Salen funnel. She was on charter to Salen to carry a full load of apples and pears to the UK and the funnel was painted whilst she was in port.
BOB SILBERBERG, 22 Ernest Street, Beauty Point 7270, Tasmania, Australia

City of Melbourne (opposite) makes an interesting contrast with *City of Newcastle* (above), the ship to which she was originally to be a sister. The *City of Montreal* is almost 30 feet longer, but forward of the superstructure the ships are very similar. [William Riddell; Alex Duncan]

Comments and corrections

Record 24:

The article on the 'Big ics' induced waves of pleasant nostalgia. My father worked for the local Shaw Savill agents here, so when the *Corinthic* arrived on her maiden voyage I was given a pass to explore her from stem to stern - the first deep-sea ship I had ever boarded. Similar visits followed as the *Athenic* and *Ceramic* as they arrived. Subsequently the Auckland Maritime Society had a very pleasant evening on the *Athenic,* just before her passenger accommodation was removed - I had the job of providing the main talk which dealt with the Aberdeen Line as I had already done Shaw Savill and Albion itself at a similar function on the *Dominion Monarch* just before she was broken up.

Page 207. *Dunadd:* Should the Celtic kingdom not be Dalriada, rather than Dalrinda? Dalriada was the ancient Celtic kingdom covering the Kintyre peninsula and parts of Argyll after which the centenary steamer of the Campbeltown and Glasgow Steam Packet Joint Stock Company was named (*Dalriada* 758/1926).

Page 212: *Mabel Warwick:* Should it not be W.C., rather than S.C., Warwick?

Pages 213-4: The twin engines in *Oredia, Orelia, Oreosa* and *Orepton* were of Gray-Polar design.

Record 25:

Page 8: *Beaverlake* was sold to Costa in 1962, not 1952.

Page 18: *Mount Manisty* was ex HS 30, not HS 31.

Page 38: *Salerno* was built in 1882, not 1888, and for R.W. Jones and Co. of Newport, not Scruttons who did not acquire her until 1883.

Page 55: *Iron Chief* was not a tanker, nor was she Norwegian. As her name implies, she was an ore carrier, built by Doxfords in 1930 for Interstate Steamships Ltd of Sydney.

BILL LAXON, Waimarama, Upper Whangateau Road, PO Box 171, Matakana 1240, New Zealand.

A.D. Frost points out that we should have been aware of the true nature of the Iron Chief: *on page 61 our publication 'Feilden's Mersey' mentions how she replaced a more conventional tramp carrying the same name. Ed.*

On the bottle

A brief note to thank you and the 'Ships in Focus' production team for *Record* 24. The use of colour was not only exceptionally generous this time but I particularly enjoyed the opportunity you took to introduce the old bottle, new wine concept and to showcase Louis Loughran's funnels expertise. I trust that we can look forward to a repetition of both of these features? Three comments which might be of interest.

The *Otagold* on page 228 may well have been on her way to the breakers when photographed but that does make a small mystery of the scaffolding platforms rigged just under the crosstrees on every mast. What's going on here? My experience tells me that the derrick head blocks are going to receive their quadrennial inspection but this hardly squares with an imminent appointment with the blowtorches of Kaoshiung. Maybe some prior dismantling was going on before a sale was finalised ?

The comment (page 260) made by Vic Matthews about the bow device on the *Orecrest* rings true. As Ivanovic the manager was a pre-war Yugoslav shipowner then the 'Freedom' tag was presumably a barbed comment on the fate of his country at the time. It would have played well with any Yugoslav exiles who then worked in the Canadian ore-loading ports.

The marvellous illustrations of Garston Docks are a real find. My father spent most of his working life there with Elders and Fyffes, he was the man who planned the allocation of stems to each railway van (not many LGVs around in his lifetime). I wonder if the photograph on page 248 shows the man who made the classic remark, reported with relish by my father, 'make an aperture in them vans so's the men can percolate through' on one morning when the labour could not get onto the ship due to some clumsy marshalling on the quay. Needless to say, this remark then had to be translated somewhat before any action appeared to correct matters.

JOHN GOBLE, 55 Shanklin Road, Southampton SO15 7RG

Sunderland in and out of focus

Thanks are due to your Editor for including two additional photographs in my second 'Sunderland in Focus' article (*Record* 25), neither of which I had seen before! That on page 53, of course, is just one of the thousands taken over the years from that, 'south-east corner of Wearmouth Bridge' vantage point highlighted in 'Sunderland in Focus 1' (*Record* 19), and which was the starting point of this mini-series. As the caption states, one of the vessels shown in the photograph is *Mr. Therm* returning to her builder's yard having had her engines installed at North Eastern Marine's works in the South Dock, and, of interest, in the charge of two Lambton, Hetton and Joicey Collieries tugs, with the third unit of that fleet moored alongside the famous Austin's pontoon, awaiting her next orders. *Clanwood,* shown on the pontoon, was one of four similar vessels ordered by France, Fenwick after the Great War from builders not usually involved in collier building (Vickers at Barrow, and Sir James Laing at Sunderland). In an attempt to eliminate the costly damage to the shaft tunnel regularly sustained during loading/discharge of midship-engined colliers, these ships were built with the tunnel top carried out to the ship's side, with the resulting space underneath used for water ballast. Unfortunately no one had checked the effect that this, otherwise good idea, might have on stability, and the vessels' proved to be extremely tender when loaded, so much so that after a short period in service, they had to be modified by having the tanks removed.

I must confess that the second addition, that of *Forestash* launching from the Swan, Hunter Southwick yard, is the first photograph I have ever seen of that shipyard in use, and is of particular interest for showing that the building berths were partly served by travelling cranes. Elsewhere in the yard, where conventional derricks were still in use, they are clearly of a more sophisticated design than adopted in other yards. Readers looking to 'tie-in' this photograph with others in the article showing the geography of the river, may have noted the structure of the Queen Alexandra Bridge standing above *Stottpool,* and the slopes of the ballast hill separating the Pickersgill and Priestman yards, looming over the stern of James Irwing's tug.

Having praised the Editor for the inclusion of these photographs, he must be chided for some over-enthusiastic re-writing on page 57, which transposed Osbourne, Graham's delivery of naval tonnage into the *Second World War.* Obviously, since the yard closed in the mid-twenties, these vessels were built during the Great War!

JOHN LINGWOOD, 52 Nursery Road, Sunderland SR3 1NT

Garston dredgers and *Pays De Waes*

What splendid photos and captions in Nigel Bowker's 'special' on Garston in *Record* 24, and it is tempting to try to identify the small number of London, Midland and Scottish Railway port craft which Nigel leaves nameless. By reference to the Liverpool-registered units of LMS in the 1932 Shipowners supplement to 'Lloyd's Register', the elderly hopper (assumed) in Old Dock on page 243 is possibly *Stratton* (383/1902 and 153.5 feet), built by C.H. Walker of Sudbrook. She was the oldest in the fleet at that time. By the time we reach New Dock on page 249, Nigel seems to have run out of steam a little (!) as he offers no name for the large four-grab dredger lying across the centre of the photo. The largest in the Garston fleet appears to be *Rhyl* (988/1911 and 200 feet) built by Ferguson Brothers at Port Glasgow and described in the main register as a 'suction and grab hopper dredger'. An alternative would be *North Western* (874/1908 and 190 feet), also by Ferguson and described as a 'grab hopper dredger'. Duckworth and Langmuir in 'Railway and Other Steamers' have both of these disposed of in 1950, while the old *Stratton* went to Ardrossan breakers in 1935. Perhaps *Record* can search out some photos of these vessels for comparison?

Way back in *Record* 14, Ian Farquhar covered 'Australian Two-Funnellers' and included in his article *Indarra* from William Denny in 1912 for Australasian United Steam Navigation. Her Australian coastal service being cut short by